EYEWITNESS SCIENCE

LIGHT

Late 19th-century "fusees" used to light cigars

Primitive oil-burning shell lamp

Jealousy glass c.1780, used to view the audience at the theater

Gregorian telescope c.1760

Beeswax candle and late 19th-century brass holder

Modern color slides

Iron glasses with horn rims c.1750

Magic lantern c.1895, used to project colored images

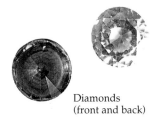
Diamonds
(front and back)

EYEWITNESS ◉ SCIENCE

Compact disc

LIGHT

Written by
DAVID BURNIE

Geissler tube used
for lighting

Reflecting cat's eye

Barton's button c.1830

Cutaway refracting telescope

Coronet Midget
camera c.1934

Primary and
secondary colors

DK

DORLING KINDERSLEY, INC.
NEW YORK

Woolaston optometer
c.1830, used to test
the eye's ability to focus

Newton's rings,
1870, used to
demonstrate
interference

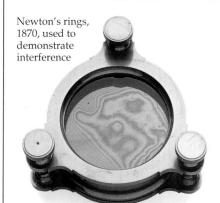

DK

A DORLING KINDERSLEY BOOK

👉 **NOTE TO PARENTS AND TEACHERS**
The **Eyewitness Science** series encourages children
to observe and question the world around them. It will help
families to answer their questions about why and how things
work—from daily occurrences in the home to the mysteries
of space. In school, these books are a valuable resource.
Teachers will find them useful for work in many subjects,
and the experiments and demonstrations in the book 👉
can serve as an inspiration for classroom activities.

Project Editor Stephanie Jackson
Designer Gurinder Purewall
Design Assistant Marianna Papachrysanthou
DTP Manager Joanna Figg-Latham
Production Eunice Paterson
Managing Editor Josephine Buchanan
Senior Art Editor Neville Graham
Special Photography Dave King
US Editor Charles A. Wills
US Consultant Harvey B. Loomis

First American Edition, 1992
10 9 8 7 6 5 4 3 2 1

First published in the United States by
Dorling Kindersley, Inc., 232 Madison Avenue,
New York, New York 10016

Plane mirror
c.1870

Library of Congress Cataloging–in–Publication Data
Burnie, David.
    Light / David Burnie. — 1st American ed.
      p   cm. — (Eyewitness science)
    Includes index.
    Summary: A guide to the origins, principles, and historical study
of light.
    ISBN 1-879431-79-3
    1. Light—Juvenile literature.   [1. Light.] I. Title.
II. Series.
QC360.B87   1992
535—dc20
                                    92-7661
                                    CIP
                                    AC

Mid 19th-century
hand polariscope
used to show
polarization
of different
substances

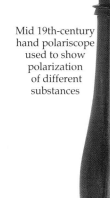

Reproduced by Colourscan, Singapore
Printed and bound in Italy by A. Mondadori Editore, Verona

Replica of
Newton's
telescope

Contents

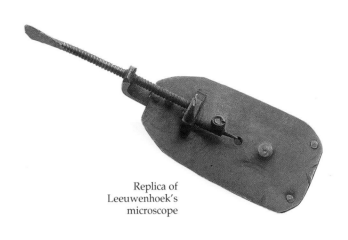

Replica of
Leeuwenhoek's
microscope

Light, myth, and magic

IMAGINE WHAT WOULD happen to the earth if tomorrow the sun did not rise. Within hours it would become as cold as winter. After a few days ponds and rivers would begin to freeze, and plants and animals would start to die. Soon, oil would turn solid, and engines would not work. Power station generators would come to a standstill. There would be no way to transport food to stores, or to bring it home. Unless fuel could be found to make a fire, there would be no light or heat.

But could this ever happen? With current knowledge of the solar system, it is certain that the answer is no. But in the past people could not be so certain. They had no clear idea of how the sun produced light or why it moved through the sky. By worshiping the sun as a god, they guarded against it going out.

FROM HEAT TO LIGHT
Lightning is produced when an electric spark makes air so hot that it glows. In nature most forms of light are brought about by heat.

LURING LIGHT
The eerie "Will o' the wisp" is a naturally occurring flame that can occur over marshy ground. The flame's fuel is methane, a gas produced by rotting plants. The methane bubbles rise to the surface together with phosphine, a gas from the rotting remains of animals. Phosphine ignites when it meets air, lighting the methane. The quickly moving flame is almost impossible to follow.

Replica of an Inca sun mask

LIVELY LIGHT
Legends and folklore are full of spirits, apparitions, and sea monsters that glow in the dark. Many of these "sightings" are probably due to plants and animals that can make their own light (p. 45). Living things, like this planktonic fish, use these lights to confuse their enemies, find a mate, or lure food toward them.

LIGHT FROM ABOVE
In the far North and South, the night sky sometimes lights up with beautiful curtains of light known as "auroras." They occur when tiny electrically charged particles from the sun collide with atoms in the earth's atmosphere. The earth's magnetic field draws the particles toward the North and South Poles. The name "aurora" is the Latin word for "dawn."

THE SPLENDOR OF THE SUN
This golden mask is a replica of one made by the Incas in Ecuador. The Incas worshiped the sun and believed that their rulers were the sun's living descendants.

THE SUN IN STONE
This stone face once stared out from a great pyramid built in the 16th century by the Aztecs of Mexico. It stood in the Aztec capital city, Tenochtitlan, which was built on islands in Lake Texcoco. It is a "calendar stone," showing the sun god Tonatiuh surrounded by symbols of the universe and the days of the year. The triangle pointing outward represents the sun's rays. Such stones were used not only as calendars, but also to help predict when solar eclipses would occur.

THE SUN IN ANCIENT EGYPT
This scene is from the throne of the Egyptian pharaoh Tutankhamen, who lived about 1350 BC. Tutankhamen's father-in-law swept away all the traditional gods and replaced them with one – Aton, the sun god. When Tutankhamen came to the throne he restored the old gods, but Aton remained the most important.

FACING THE LIGHT
In ancient times people did not know about photosynthesis – the process by which plants use light (p. 50). But they could see that plants needed light because leaves and flowers grow so that they face the light, and they often turn to follow the sun's changing position through the day. The sunflower was used in sun worship in Central and South America. It gets its English name from its sunlike face. In French, it is called "tournesol," meaning "turn towards the sun."

IMPERIAL SUN
This sun symbol is found at the City Palace, Jaipur, India. It is thought to be the imperial symbol of the family of the 18th-century warrior-astronomer Maharajah Jai Singh, whose leader was known as the "Sun of the Hindus." In 1728 he began building a complex outdoor observatory, the Jantar Mantar, which is still in use in Jaipur. It contains a massive sundial.

7

Making light

At some time in the distant past, humans learned how to harness fire. At first, fire was something they had to find and collect. They would light piles of branches from bushfires and keep them blazing for as long as they could. If the flames went out, the search for new fire had to begin again. Later, people discovered ways to make fires themselves. By striking stones together, or rubbing wood against wood, they could make sparks or generate enough heat to set fire to dry tinder. Once they had mastered this, they could have light and heat whenever they wanted.

FIRE FROM ABOVE
According to the legends of ancient Greece, the god Zeus prevented humans from having fire. However, Prometheus stole some fire from the mountain home of the gods and brought it down into the world. The "bringing of fire" stills happens today at the beginning of the Olympic Games, when a burning flame is carried from Greece to the place where the games are to be held.

Pyrites

Flint

STRIKING A LIGHT
Flint and iron pyrites are two minerals that give off sparks if they are hit with something hard. They were probably the first pieces of firemaking equipment to be used by our ancestors. To produce a flame, the sparks had to land on tinder – a dry, light material, such as wood dust, feathery plant seeds, or fungus. In later years, flint and iron pyrites were both used to ignite gunpowder in "flintlock" rifles. Older cigarette lighters also use artificial "flints" to make sparks.

FIRE PLOUGH AND HEARTH
Rubbing your hands together makes them become warm. This is because friction caused by rubbing gives rise to heat. With hands, the rise in temperature is small. But if a stick is rubbed very quickly against another piece of wood, it can become hot enough to make tinder catch fire. In this Aboriginal fire plough and hearth from Australia, the stick, or "plough," is pushed along the groove towards the "hearth." Hot pieces of the stick jump on to the tinder placed in the hearth to make a flame.

Plough

Hearth

TARRED TORCHES
Poles topped with burning tar or rags cast a bright yellow light. These flaming torches could be carried from place to place or fastened to walls. Roman cities used torches as street lighting over 2,000 years ago.

GUIDING LIGHT
The Pharos of Alexandria was the first recorded full-scale lighthouse. It was over 260 ft (80 m) high, and it used the light of burning wood to guide ships into harbor. It was completed in 280 BC, but was eventually toppled by an earthquake.

LIGHT FROM FLAMES
Light is a form of energy. When a fire is lit, chemical energy is released. The burning fuel emits gases, and the chemical energy heats the gas atoms, making them glow, or incandesce. A flame's color tells how much energy is being released, and how hot the flame is. A dull yellow flame is cooler than a bright blue one – but will still burn anything that is too close.

2,000-year-old
Egyptian pottery
oil lamp

Oil lamp from the
Orkney Islands, near Scotland

Wick soaks up oil

Shell holds oil

*Leather is used to
suspend the lamp*

LIGHT FROM OIL
In the earliest
days of fire, humans
noticed that animal fat
and plant oils burned with
a bright yellow light. This was
the first step in the invention of
the oil lamp. Oil, on its own, is not
an easily manageable source of light.
It has to be very hot before it will
burn, but when it is hot it will often
flare up very quickly. Eventually, people
learned to use a "wick" – something that
soaks up the oil so that it burns little by
little. Some of the oldest oil lamps that
have been discovered were made out of
rocks and shells about 15,000 years ago. Oil
lamps are still used today throughout the world.

THE SEARCH FOR OIL
Before gas lighting was invented, there was a great
demand for animal oil. Oil came mainly from the fat
of sea animals – whales, seals, and even penguins –
which was boiled down in huge vats to make "tallow."

Beeswax
candle

19th-century gaslights

GAS LIGHTING
During the 19th century,
gas lighting became
widespread in towns and
cities. At first, gaslights
were simply jets of burning
gas. Later, their brightness
was increased by using
a "mantle." This is a fine
net of chemically treated
fabric that fits over the
gas jet. The heat of the
gas flame causes the mantle
to give off a bright light.

19th-century
cigar-lighting
"fusees"

TRAVELING LIGHT
Matches create a flame by a chemical
reaction. Most use compounds of
phosphorus, which catch fire when exposed to air.
Early matches sometimes caught fire without being
struck at all, but more modern "safety" matches work
only when struck against the matchbox. The "fusees"
shown here were designed for lighting cigars in a breeze.

SOLID OIL LAMP
A candle is simply an oil lamp with solid oil.
Before the 1800s candles were made of
tallow or beeswax. They produced a lot of
smoke but not much light. Today, most
candles are made of paraffin wax.

Shadows

Since ancient times, people have known that light travels in straight lines. This can be seen by looking at the beam of light from a film projector. The beam is made up of many "rays" of light. Although the rays spread out in the shape of a fan, each individual ray travels in a straight line from the projector to the screen. If somebody stands up and blocks part of the beam, some of the light rays will not reach the screen, while the light rays in the rest of the beam carry on as before. The result is an area without light – a shadow.

STRAIGHT SUNBEAMS
Sunbeams show that light travels in straight lines. Sunbeams can be seen only if dust, as in this old barn, or droplets of moisture in the air scatter some of their light. The scattered light travels outward in straight lines, and some of it reaches the eyes, so that the beam can be seen.

TIME FROM THE SUN
The sun always moves across the sky at a steady rate, so if a stick is pushed vertically into the ground, the time of day can be told by seeing where its shadow lies. This is the principle of the sundial. Simple sundials were used in Egypt at least 3,000 years ago. This unusual column sundial was made in Germany in about 1550. The time is shown both on the column and on the vertical faces beneath it.

Pointer

The pointer's shadow touches a curved line that indicates the time

Compass used to set the sundial in the correct direction

Dial marked with hours

SHARP SHADOWS
Light rays fan out from a candle in straight lines to cast a shadow of anything that blocks their path. Etienne de Silhouette (1709-1767), a French government minister, used this principle to make shadow portraits that were much cheaper than paintings. Today, the name silhouette is used to describe any black shape seen against the light.

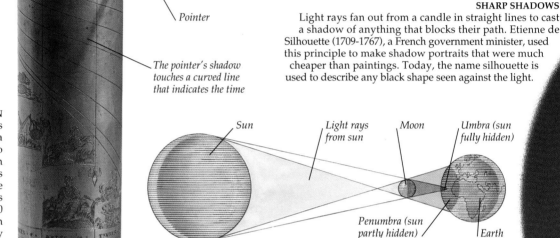

Sun — *Light rays from sun* — *Moon* — *Umbra (sun fully hidden)* — *Penumbra (sun partly hidden)* — *Earth*

SHADOWS IN SPACE
During an eclipse of the sun, the moon comes between the earth and the sun and its shadow moves across the earth. In the middle of the shadow, the "umbra," all the sun's light is blocked. Around this is the "penumbra," where only part of the sun's light is blocked. Anyone in the path of the umbra sees a "total" eclipse, in which the sun disappears. People in the path of the penumbra see a "partial" eclipse. To them, part of the sun is always visible.

PREDICTING AN ECLIPSE
When Christopher Columbus landed on Jamaica in 1504 he could not persuade the native Indians to give him enough supplies. Columbus knew that an eclipse of the moon was about to occur, so he "commanded" the moon to go dark. The Indians were so astonished by his "powers" that they gave him the help he needed.

Leonardo da Vinci

STUDYING SHADOWS
The great Italian artist and engineer Leonardo da Vinci (1452-1519) investigated almost every branch of science, including the study of light. This sketch from one of his many notebooks shows light travelling outward from a pair of candles and casting shadows on either side of an object. Beneath the drawing are some of da Vinci's notes, written in the back-to-front "mirror writing" that he often used.
Da Vinci applied his findings as a scientist to his works of art. In many of his paintings he used deep shadows to build up an image.

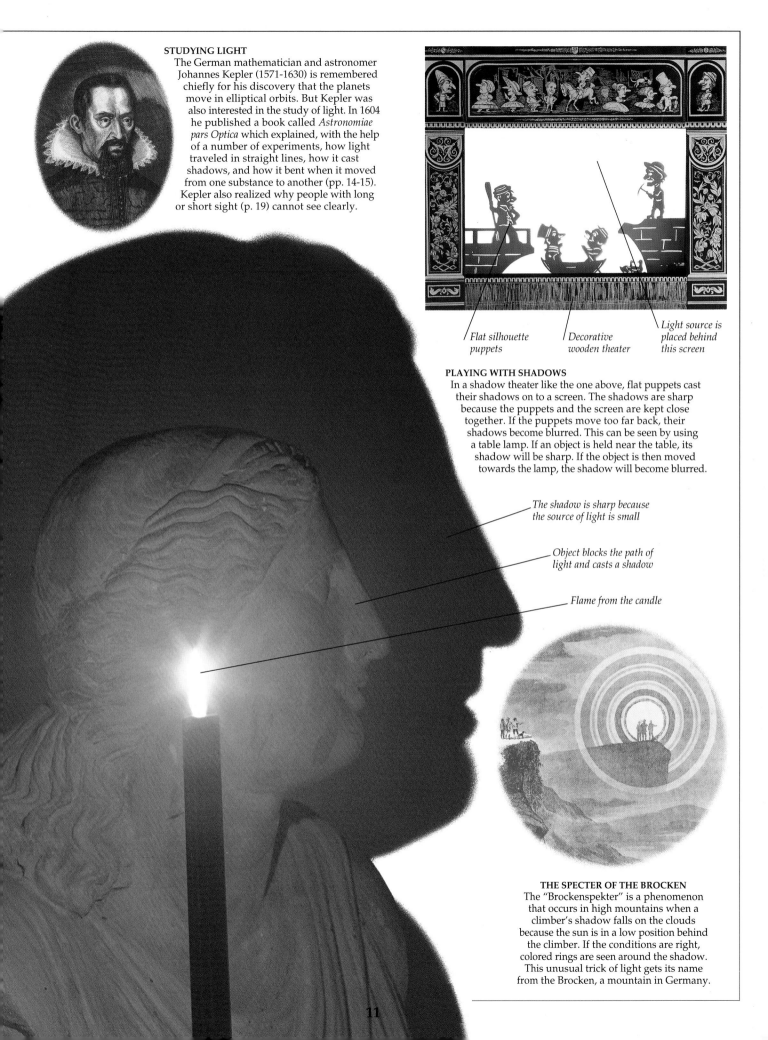

STUDYING LIGHT

The German mathematician and astronomer Johannes Kepler (1571-1630) is remembered chiefly for his discovery that the planets move in elliptical orbits. But Kepler was also interested in the study of light. In 1604 he published a book called *Astronomiae pars Optica* which explained, with the help of a number of experiments, how light traveled in straight lines, how it cast shadows, and how it bent when it moved from one substance to another (pp. 14-15). Kepler also realized why people with long or short sight (p. 19) cannot see clearly.

Flat silhouette puppets

Decorative wooden theater

Light source is placed behind this screen

PLAYING WITH SHADOWS

In a shadow theater like the one above, flat puppets cast their shadows on to a screen. The shadows are sharp because the puppets and the screen are kept close together. If the puppets move too far back, their shadows become blurred. This can be seen by using a table lamp. If an object is held near the table, its shadow will be sharp. If the object is then moved towards the lamp, the shadow will become blurred.

The shadow is sharp because the source of light is small

Object blocks the path of light and casts a shadow

Flame from the candle

THE SPECTER OF THE BROCKEN

The "Brockenspekter" is a phenomenon that occurs in high mountains when a climber's shadow falls on the clouds because the sun is in a low position behind the climber. If the conditions are right, colored rings are seen around the shadow. This unusual trick of light gets its name from the Brocken, a mountain in Germany.

11

Reflecting light

W<small>HEN A RAY</small> of light hits a mirror it is reflected, meaning that it bounces back. This can be seen by looking at the surface of a pool of water, just as people would have done long ago. As long as the water's surface is smooth, light is reflected in an orderly way and there is a clear image. But if the water becomes ruffled by the wind, light is reflected in many different directions. Instead of a clear image, there is now a jumble of scattered light. It is known that the ancient Greek mathematician Euclid understood how light is reflected. As long ago as 300 BC, he investigated how reflection takes place, and so did a number of Greek scientists who followed him. But it was not until the 1100s that the Arab scientist Alhazen pieced together the law that describes exactly what happens to a ray of light when it strikes a surface and then bounces off it.

MIRRORED IN WATER
The surface of still water makes a natural mirror. According to Greek mythology, a youth called Narcissus fell in love with his own reflection in a pool of water. When he tried to reach the reflection, he fell into the water and drowned.

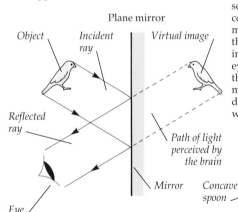

EARLY MIRROR
This Egyptian bronze mirror was made in about 1300 BC. The bronze was highly polished to give a clear reflection. Glass mirrors date back many centuries, but mirrors of clear glass first appeared in Venice in about AD 1300. Like today's mirrors, they were backed by a very thin layer of metal, which reflected light.

CURVED AND FLAT SURFACES (below and right)
The kind of reflection that is seen in a mirror depends on its shape and how far away things are. Here are reflections from flat, or "plane," concave, and convex surfaces.

REFLECTIONS AND IMAGES
Reflection always involves two rays – an incoming, or "incident," ray and an outgoing, or "reflected," ray. The law of reflection states that the two rays are at identical angles but on opposite sides of the "normal" – an imaginary line at right angles to the mirror, through the point where the rays meet. When an object is viewed in a mirror, the eyes take in light rays that have been reflected. But the brain assumes that the light rays have reached the eyes in straight lines. The brain works backward along the light paths and perceives an image behind the mirror. This "virtual" image does not really exist because it does not actually produce light. The other kind of image, one that produces light, is known as a "real" image. A real image can be thrown onto a screen (pp. 24-25), but a virtual image cannot.

Plane mirror

Object *Incident ray* *Virtual image*

Reflected ray

Path of light perceived by the brain

Mirror *Concave spoon*

Eye

Concave mirrors make objects look smaller and upside-down, unless they are very close

CONCAVE MIRRORS
When parallel light rays strike a concave mirror, which is curved inward, they are reflected in so that they come together, or converge. What is seen in a concave mirror depends on its distance from the object being reflected. If the inside of a spoon is held close to the eye, a magnified, upright view of the eye will be seen. If the spoon is moved away, a miniature, upside-down view of the whole face will be seen.

Concave mirror

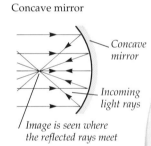

Concave mirror

Incoming light rays

Image is seen where the reflected rays meet

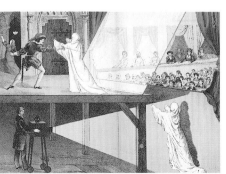

GHOSTLY APPEARANCE
If viewed from certain angles, glass on its own can act as a mirror. In the past this was used to create "ghosts" on stage. The ghost was actually an actor under the stage. An angled plane of glass reflected light from the ghost towards the audience. They would see the ghost, but not the glass.

Because the apple is so close to this concave bowl, a large, upright image is formed

Concave bowl

CONVEX MIRRORS

A convex mirror bulges outward. When parallel light rays strike the mirror, they are reflected so that they spread out, or diverge. When someone looks into a convex mirror, their brain traces back along the rays as if they were coming from behind the mirror. A small, upright "virtual" image of anything reflected in the mirror is seen. Because convex mirrors give a wide view, they are used in cars. They make things look small, so drivers must remember that things in a rearview mirror may be closer than they seem.

The cylindrical mirror reflects a perfectly shaped image

Convex mirror

Incoming light ray

Reflected light ray

Virtual image is seen behind the mirror

Convex mirror

Convex cup

Upright images are formed of all the objects in a wide area

CHANGING SHAPE

This painting of a butterfly looks strange and distorted. But when it is reflected in a cylindrical mirror, it becomes perfectly shaped. Paintings like this are examples of "anamorphic" toys, which were very popular in the 18th and 19th centuries. Anamorphic artists worked by looking at the mirror, rather than the paper.

Anamorphic butterfly, 1870

Concave–convex dish

Cut diamonds

Front view sparkles

Rear view is dark

BOUNCING BACK

A cut diamond is designed to reflect most of the light that falls on its front. Some of the light is reflected by the outside of the diamond's upper faces and some by the inside of the lower faces. This is why a diamond sparkles when viewed from the front but is dull when seen from behind.

Observer looks here

Plane mirror set at 45° gives a sideways view

Distorted images are formed by the changing curves of this surface

False front

The flat part of the plate is a plane mirror that forms a clear image of anything reflected in it

PLANE MIRRORS

A flat, or "plane," mirror reflects objects without distorting them. Although the image is the right way up, it is back-to-front or left-right reversed. Police cars and ambulances often have back-to-front signs, which look the right way around when seen in a car mirror.

Plane mirror

Incoming light ray

Plane mirror

Reflected light ray

SEEING SIDEWAYS

This polemoscope, or "jealousy glass," was made in 1780. It was designed to make it look as though the person using it was looking forward, but in fact it contains a plane mirror that gives a sideways view. Jealousy glasses were used in theaters by people who wanted to keep a close eye on the audience rather than the entertainment.

Bending light

WHEN LIGHT PASSES FROM ONE SUBSTANCE to another it is bent, or "refracted." One way to see refraction is to put something in a glass of water. Its shape will seem to change because the light rays bend as they leave the water and enter the air. People have known about refraction for a long time. Early scientists realized that it was a precise effect and tried to make a mathematical law to show how much bending occurred. The Egyptian geographer Ptolemy (AD 90-168) probably devised the first "law of refraction." It worked in some cases, but was unreliable. Alhazen (p. 12) investigated refraction but could not predict how far light would bend. The problem was solved in 1621 by Willebrord Snell, and his law is still known as "Snell's Law."

WISHFUL THINKING
Ptolemy carried out several experiments to investigate how far light was bent. He devised a law to explain the amount of refraction, but even his own results did not always agree with his law.

Light ray

Rod

Rod seems to be bent

Glass filled with water

Ray of light is bent as it leaves the air and enters the left face of the block

Clear glass block

Light inside the block travels in a straight line

BENT BUT UNBROKEN
This glass rod seems to be made of separate parts, all at different angles. This happens because light from different parts of the rod passes through different combinations of water, glass, and air. Each time it moves from one substance to another, it is bent.

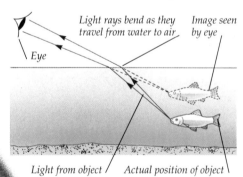

Light rays bend as they travel from water to air

Image seen by eye

Eye

Light from object   *Actual position of object*

HOW DEEP IS IT?
When an object is seen in water, the light rays from it are bent as they travel from water to air. The eyes follow the rays back as though they had traveled in straight lines, so a "virtual" image (p. 12) is seen. This image is not as deep as the object.

SNELL'S LAW OF REFRACTION
In this experiment a beam of light is bent as it enters and leaves a clear glass block. When the beam hits the block, it turns more steeply toward it – the beam shown here becomes more horizontal. When it leaves the block, it is bent again in the opposite direction. The amount of bending is very precise. If the beam enters or leaves the block head-on, it will not be bent at all. If it enters or leaves at any other angle, it will be bent, and the bending increases as the beam gets further from the head-on position. In 1621 the Dutch mathematician and astronomer Willebrord Snell found there was a characteristic ratio between a beam's "angle of incidence" (its angle before bending) and its "angle of refraction" (its angle after bending). His law shows that every substance has a characteristic bending power – its "refractive index." The more a substance bends light, the larger its refractive index.

WILLEBRORD SNELL
Willebrord Snell (1580-1626) discovered one of the most important laws concerning light. He also pioneered triangulation, a way to measure distances by using the angles between different points.

As it leaves the block and enters the air, the light is bent back again

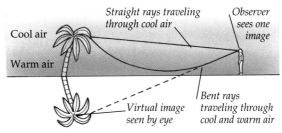

Cool air
Warm air

Straight rays traveling through cool air
Observer sees one image
Bent rays traveling through cool and warm air
Virtual image seen by eye

MIRAGES

A mirage occurs when a layer of warm air next to the ground is trapped by cooler air above. Light is bent toward the horizontal line of vision and eventually it is made to travel upward by total internal reflection (p. 54). The mirage is an upside-down "virtual" image (p. 12).

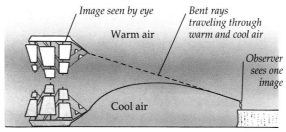

Image seen by eye
Bent rays traveling through warm and cool air
Warm air
Observer sees one image
Cool air

LOOMING

In this form of mirage, warm air lies over a layer of cold air. The light rays traveling from cold to warm air are bent toward the horizontal line of vision and eventually reflected downward. As a result, an object seems to "loom" above its real position.

SCHLIEREN PHOTOGRAPHY

Air at different temperatures bends light by different amounts. Schlieren photography is a way of making these differences easy to see. It works by blocking some of the light coming from the object, so that the bent light becomes more visible. Above is a Schlieren photograph of a candle. It shows layers of air at different temperatures around the flame.

BENDING BY AIR

Light rays can sometimes be bent without passing from one substance to another. In air this happens when light travels through layers that are at different temperatures. Cold air is more dense and heavier than light air, so it acts like a different substance. The results can be spectacular, as this old engraving shows.

CONCENTRATING LIGHT

These water-filled spheres are known as lacemaker's condensers. They were made in the early 19th century and were used by lacemakers to help them see their work. When light travels through the glass spheres, it is bent in a way that makes it fall on a small area of the lace. The condenser concentrates, or "focuses," the light.

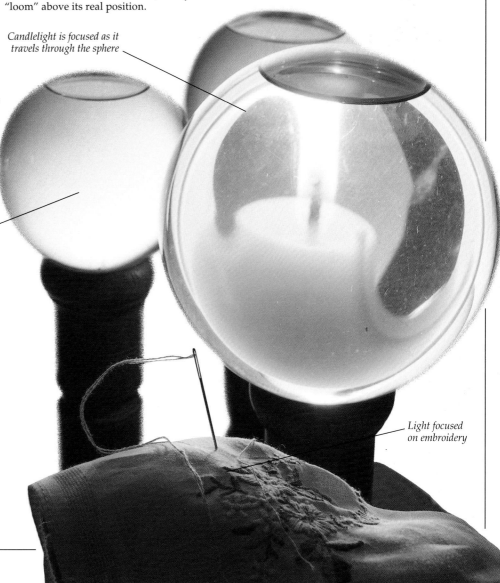

Candlelight is focused as it travels through the sphere

Each condenser focuses light on a different area

Light focused on embroidery

HOW THE CONDENSER WORKS

When light rays travel through a curved surface, some rays are bent more than others. A lacemaker's condenser focuses the rays so that they meet in a small area. The condenser acts like a convex lens (pp. 14-15).

Looking through lenses

LATIN LENTILS
The word "lens" comes from the Latin name for lentils. A lentil seed is flat and round, and its sides bulge outward – just like a convex lens.

IF YOU LOOK through a window, everything beyond it seems about the same as it would without the window there. But if you look through a glass of water, what you see is very different. The view is distorted, and it may be reversed. The reason for this is that the glass of water acts like a lens; it bends the light rays that pass through it. There are two main types of lens. A convex, or converging, lens curves outward, and makes light bend inward. A concave lens is just the opposite: it curves inward, and makes light bend outward. If parallel rays of light strike a convex lens head-on, they are bent so that they all pass through one place – the "principal focus." The distance from the principal focus to the center of the lens is called the "focal distance." The shorter this distance, the more powerful the lens.

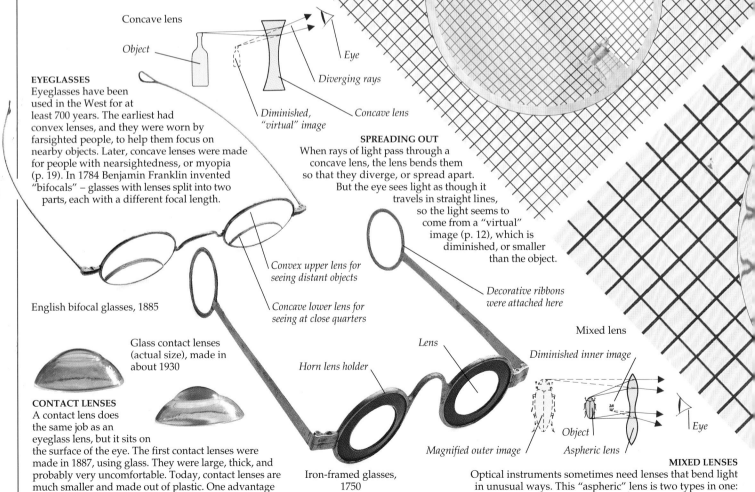

Concave lens

Object

Eye

Diverging rays

Diminished, "virtual" image

Concave lens

EYEGLASSES
Eyeglasses have been used in the West for at least 700 years. The earliest had convex lenses, and they were worn by farsighted people, to help them focus on nearby objects. Later, concave lenses were made for people with nearsightedness, or myopia (p. 19). In 1784 Benjamin Franklin invented "bifocals" – glasses with lenses split into two parts, each with a different focal length.

SPREADING OUT
When rays of light pass through a concave lens, the lens bends them so that they diverge, or spread apart. But the eye sees light as though it travels in straight lines, so the light seems to come from a "virtual" image (p. 12), which is diminished, or smaller than the object.

English bifocal glasses, 1885

Convex upper lens for seeing distant objects

Concave lower lens for seeing at close quarters

Decorative ribbons were attached here

Mixed lens

Diminished inner image

Lens

Glass contact lenses (actual size), made in about 1930

Horn lens holder

Object

Eye

Magnified outer image

Aspheric lens

CONTACT LENSES
A contact lens does the same job as an eyeglass lens, but it sits on the surface of the eye. The first contact lenses were made in 1887, using glass. They were large, thick, and probably very uncomfortable. Today, contact lenses are much smaller and made out of plastic. One advantage of contact lenses is that, unlike eyeglasses, they allow clear vision across the whole of the eye's field of view.

Iron-framed glasses, 1750

MIXED LENSES
Optical instruments sometimes need lenses that bend light in unusual ways. This "aspheric" lens is two types in one: it is convex near its edges, but concave at the center. Lenses like this are used in rangefinders and weapons systems.

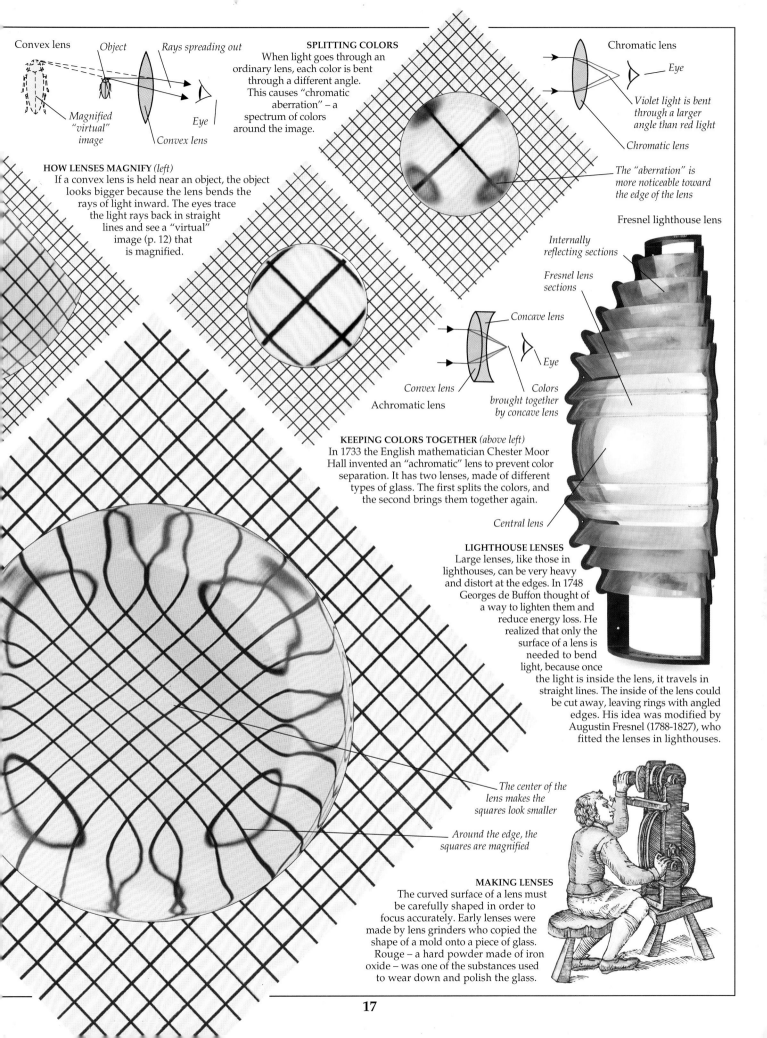

Convex lens

Object

Rays spreading out

Magnified "virtual" image

Eye

Convex lens

HOW LENSES MAGNIFY (*left*)
If a convex lens is held near an object, the object looks bigger because the lens bends the rays of light inward. The eyes trace the light rays back in straight lines and see a "virtual" image (p. 12) that is magnified.

SPLITTING COLORS
When light goes through an ordinary lens, each color is bent through a different angle. This causes "chromatic aberration" – a spectrum of colors around the image.

Chromatic lens

Eye

Violet light is bent through a larger angle than red light

Chromatic lens

The "aberration" is more noticeable toward the edge of the lens

Fresnel lighthouse lens

Internally reflecting sections

Fresnel lens sections

Concave lens

Eye

Convex lens

Colors brought together by concave lens

Achromatic lens

KEEPING COLORS TOGETHER (*above left*)
In 1733 the English mathematician Chester Moor Hall invented an "achromatic" lens to prevent color separation. It has two lenses, made of different types of glass. The first splits the colors, and the second brings them together again.

Central lens

LIGHTHOUSE LENSES
Large lenses, like those in lighthouses, can be very heavy and distort at the edges. In 1748 Georges de Buffon thought of a way to lighten them and reduce energy loss. He realized that only the surface of a lens is needed to bend light, because once the light is inside the lens, it travels in straight lines. The inside of the lens could be cut away, leaving rings with angled edges. His idea was modified by Augustin Fresnel (1788-1827), who fitted the lenses in lighthouses.

The center of the lens makes the squares look smaller

Around the edge, the squares are magnified

MAKING LENSES
The curved surface of a lens must be carefully shaped in order to focus accurately. Early lenses were made by lens grinders who copied the shape of a mold onto a piece of glass. Rouge – a hard powder made of iron oxide – was one of the substances used to wear down and polish the glass.

Seeing light images

HOW EXACTLY DO THE EYES WORK? Until about AD 1000 it was widely believed that the eyes gave out light, and that the light somehow formed a picture. People thought that if a hand was put in front of them, there would be no image because the light would not be able to come out. But in about 1020, the Arab scientist Alhazen correctly suggested that things work the other way around – that the eyes take in light, rather than give it out. During the following centuries, doctors and scientists made detailed studies of the eye's structure. They learned that the eye's lens throws an image onto a living screen, called the retina. Thanks to the invention of the microscope (pp. 22-23), it is now known that the retina is packed with light-sensitive cells that send messages through the optic nerve to the brain.

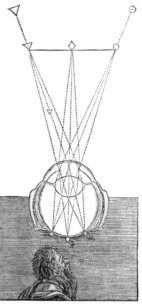

MAKING AN IMAGE
In the 17th century the French philosopher and mathematician René Descartes explained how the eye forms an image on the retina. This is one of his drawings. Instead of myths or magic, he used simple physical principles to find out what happens to light once it enters the eyeball.

The eyeball is surrounded by the sclera – a hard, white, protective layer

Muscles linking eye and eye socket

Pupil

Cornea

Blood vessels

Optic nerve */Bone at bottom of eye socket*

INSIDE AN EYE
This model human eye, made in France in about 1870, shows the different parts that make up this complicated and sensitive organ. The eye sits inside a bony cup called the eye socket. It is crisscrossed by tiny blood vessels that keep it supplied with oxygen. Pairs of muscles link the eye to the eye socket. When a muscle contracts, the eye swivels in its socket. At the back of the eye is the optic nerve ,which takes electrical signals to the brain. At the front is the cornea, a clear protective layer. Behind the cornea is the pupil, an opening that lets in light.

The pupil is smallest in bright light

The iris is made up of a ring of muscle that controls the size of the pupil

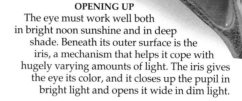

OPENING UP
The eye must work well both in bright noon sunshine and in deep shade. Beneath its outer surface is the iris, a mechanism that helps it cope with hugely varying amounts of light. The iris gives the eye its color, and it closes up the pupil in bright light and opens it wide in dim light.

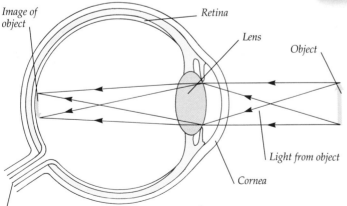

Image of object

Retina

Lens

Object

Light from object

Cornea

Optic nerve

HOW THE EYE FORMS IMAGES
The eye forms an image the same way as a camera (pp. 24-25). Light travels through the lens and is focused on the retina, which is full of light-sensitive nerve endings. When light strikes them they transmit signals through the optic nerve to the brain. The retinal image is upside-down, but, partly because it is that way from birth, the brain properly analyzes the signal.

THE BLIND SPOT
Although it is not often noticeable, one part of the retina cannot detect light. This is the area where fibers from all the different light-sensitive nerve endings join together to form the optic nerve.

Blind spot where optic nerve meets retina

Back of an eyeball

*Sliding object to test
focusing ability of the eye*

Eyepiece

Handle

MEASURING UP THE EYES
This "optometer," made
in the 19th century, was a
simple instrument that
measured the eye's
refraction (p. 14). By doing
this, an optician could select
lenses to correct defects of
vision. A modern optometrist
will examine the eyes in
many different ways. Tests
establish the shapes of the eyes
and characteristics of their lenses.
The tests will also show if some
colors are seen better than others.

LONG AND SHORT SIGHT
This 14th-century monk is wearing spectacles
to correct an eye condition that is common in
older people – farsightedness, or presbyopia. In
this defect of vision, the lens does not bend
light from nearby objects enough. The rays
meet the retina before they have been brought
into focus, and the result is a blurred image.
Nearsightedness, or myopia, occurs when the
lens bends light from distant objects too much,
and the rays meet before they hit the retina. A
third kind of defect, called astigmatism, results
in part of the image being blurred. It is caused
by the cornea not being the right shape.

Lens

*The spaces between the lens, the iris, and
the cornea are filled with a clear fluid*

*Ciliary muscles
contract to
make the lens
thicker and
relax to make
it thinner*

THE LENS REVEALED
In this model eye, the iris hinges
away to show the lens beneath. The
lens is made of a substance like hard
jelly, and its shape is changed by
tiny muscles. When the eye looks at
any object, the muscles pull the lens,
making it flatter. This changes the
focal length, and the object is
brought into focus on the retina.

*Tiny blood vessels
and nerves run over
the surfaces of the eye*

*These glands make tears to
keep the eye's surface moist*

COMPOUND EYES
The human eye has a single lens and
screen of light-sensitive nerve endings.
Many insects have "compound" eyes,
which are divided into hundreds or
thousands of compartments. Each
compartment is an individual eye with
its own lens. On their own, these eyes
cannot see much detail, but the insect's
brain adds their signals together to
build up an image. The compound
eyes of this horsefly cover most of its
head. Their brilliant colors are due to
an effect called interference (pp. 38-39).

Bringing things closer

No one knows who first discovered that a pair of lenses could be used to make distant objects look closer. According to one story, the breakthrough was made accidentally in 1608 by Hans Lippershey, a Dutch spectacle-maker, or his assistant. However, at least two other people, including Zacharias Janssen (p. 22), also claimed the discovery as theirs. What is certain is that Lippershey was quick to see the value of the "telescope," as it later became known. He applied to the Dutch government for a patent, hoping to prevent anyone else from making and selling his invention. But his request was turned down. Within just a few months, telescopes were being made and demonstrated all over Europe.

UNAIDED VIEW
Seen with the naked eye, the moon looks very small. This is because light rays from its edges reach the eye close together.

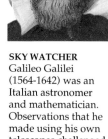

SKY WATCHER
Galileo Galilei (1564-1642) was an Italian astronomer and mathematician. Observations that he made using his own telescopes challenged beliefs of the time about the movements of the planets.

Galileo's telescope (replica)

Sliding tube for focusing

Eyepiece

Objective lens

Refracting telescopes

The first telescopes were all "refractors." Refracting telescopes use lenses to make light bend. A simple refractor has two lenses – a large objective lens with a long focal length at the end of the telescope, and a smaller eyepiece lens with a short focal length into which the observer looks. The objective lens gathers the light rays from a distant object and then bends them to form an upside-down "real" image (p. 12). Light rays from this image pass through the eyepiece lens, and are bent again so that they become parallel. Because the eye cannot tell that the light has been bent, the distant object looks bigger.

GALILEO'S TELESCOPE (*above*)
In 1609 news reached Galileo of the telescopes that were being made in Holland, and he immediately set to work building his own. This is a replica of one of the earliest that he made. It contains two lenses – a convex objective lens, and a smaller concave eyepiece lens (in other telescopes the eyepiece lens is often convex). Galileo's early telescopes magnified up to 30 times, and he used them to look at the moon, the planets, and the stars. He discovered four of the moons that orbit Jupiter. He also found out that the Milky Way is made up of millions of stars that are invisible to the naked eye.

INSIDE A REFRACTING TELESCOPE
This replica of a refracting telescope follows a design that was popular during the 18th century. It has a three-lens eyepiece, and all its lenses are chromatic (p. 17) – so the image would have been blurred by fringes of color.

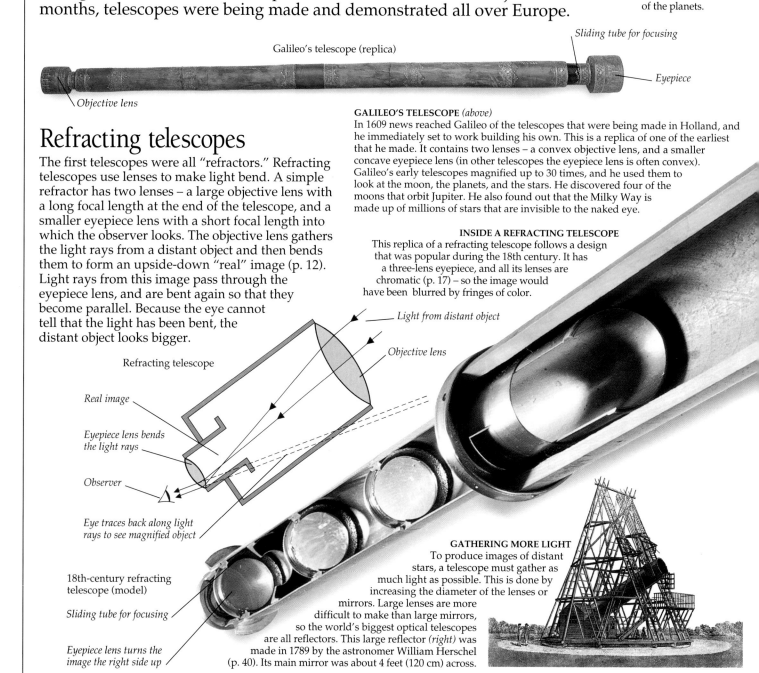

Refracting telescope

Light from distant object

Objective lens

Real image

Eyepiece lens bends the light rays

Observer

Eye traces back along light rays to see magnified object

18th-century refracting telescope (model)

Sliding tube for focusing

Eyepiece lens turns the image the right side up

GATHERING MORE LIGHT
To produce images of distant stars, a telescope must gather as much light as possible. This is done by increasing the diameter of the lenses or mirrors. Large lenses are more difficult to make than large mirrors, so the world's biggest optical telescopes are all reflectors. This large reflector (*right*) was made in 1789 by the astronomer William Herschel (p. 40). Its main mirror was about 4 feet (120 cm) across.

THE MOON BY GALILEO
In beautiful ink sketches that were published in his book *Sidereus Nuncius,* Galileo illustrated the rugged surface of the moon as he saw it through his telescope. Before he did so, many people – including scientists – thought that the moon was as smooth as a mirror.

THE MOON TODAY
Modern telescopes show the surface of the moon in great detail, with its mountain ranges and waterless "seas."

Sliding lens shield

Objective lens

Objective mirror

Secondary mirror

Observer looks here

Side view of Newton's telescope

Observer looks here

Sliding focus

Wooden ball mounting allows telescope to swivel

Reflecting telescopes
Before the invention of achromatic lenses (p. 17), color dispersion was a problem with large refractors. In 1668 Isaac Newton designed a "reflecting" telescope that avoided this problem. Instead of relying on lenses, it used mirrors. The incoming light is gathered by a large, curved mirror, and then reflected by one or more smaller mirrors into the observer's eye. Two ways of viewing the image are by looking through a hole in the objective mirror, as in a "Cassegrain" reflector, or by looking through the side of the telescope, as in a "Newtonian" reflector. Because mirrors do not disperse colors, the image is sharper.

NEWTON'S REFLECTOR
Revolutionary though it was, Newton's reflector did not actually work very well. It was small, and its mirrors tarnished very quickly. But Newton's telescope did prove that mirrors could be used to magnify. It was the forerunner of the giant reflectors that are used in observatories today.

Replica of Newton's reflecting telescope

Incoming light

Flat mirror for "Cassegrain" reflectors

Reflecting telescope

Concave objective mirror

Flat secondary mirror for "Newtonian" reflectors

In a "Newtonian" reflector the observer looks here

In a "Cassegrain" reflector the observer looks here

Making things bigger

Screw for focusing

IN 1665 AN Englishman named Robert Hooke published a remarkable book called *Micrographia*, which contained detailed descriptions and drawings of "minute bodies," from flies to fleas. With the help of a recent invention, the microscope, Hooke showed things that once had been invisible. Two types were in use – the "simple" microscope, which had just one lens, and the "compound" microscope, which had two lenses or more. Hooke used a compound microscope. In contrast, Anton van Leeuwenhoek, another pioneer of microscopy, used simple microscopes with very good lenses. He made each lens himself, and his great care was rewarded with exceptional results. He made detailed studies of many tiny "animalcules," and was the first person ever to see bacteria.

SECRET LIVES
This drawing shows a life-size animal (upper right) and how Anton van Leeuwenhoek saw it using his single-lens microscope (left).

Pin for holding specimen

Lens held between two plates

Using Leeuwenhoek's microscope

LEEUWENHOEK'S MICROSCOPE
The microscope used by Anton van Leeuwenhoek (1632-1723) was a tiny instrument made of metal. Its single lens was about $\frac{1}{25}$ in (1 mm) thick, and it had such a short focal length (p. 16) that the microscope had to be held very close to the eye. The lens was fixed between two flat metal plates. The object to be viewed was placed on a pin, and this was moved by a system of screws to bring it into focus. Leeuwenhoek actually made many hundreds of simple microscopes of various designs. Their magnifying power varied from about 70 times to more than 250 times.

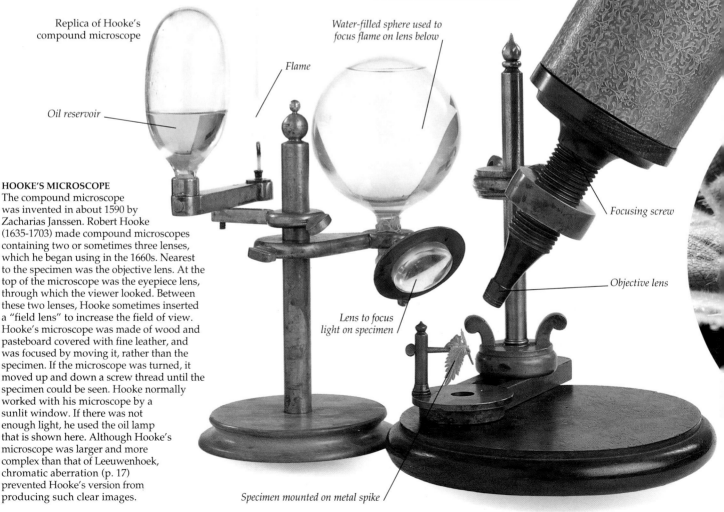

Replica of Hooke's compound microscope

Water-filled sphere used to focus flame on lens below

Flame

Oil reservoir

Focusing screw

HOOKE'S MICROSCOPE
The compound microscope was invented in about 1590 by Zacharias Janssen. Robert Hooke (1635-1703) made compound microscopes containing two or sometimes three lenses, which he began using in the 1660s. Nearest to the specimen was the objective lens. At the top of the microscope was the eyepiece lens, through which the viewer looked. Between these two lenses, Hooke sometimes inserted a "field lens" to increase the field of view. Hooke's microscope was made of wood and pasteboard covered with fine leather, and was focused by moving it, rather than the specimen. If the microscope was turned, it moved up and down a screw thread until the specimen could be seen. Hooke normally worked with his microscope by a sunlit window. If there was not enough light, he used the oil lamp that is shown here. Although Hooke's microscope was larger and more complex than that of Leeuwenhoek, chromatic aberration (p. 17) prevented Hooke's version from producing such clear images.

Lens to focus light on specimen

Objective lens

Specimen mounted on metal spike

Observer looks into eye-cup

Eyepiece lens inside base of eye-cup

Pasteboard barrel

AN INVISIBLE WORLD
Robert Hooke's great skill as an artist is shown in this view of a nettle leaf with its stinging spines. This illustration is one of the many published in *Micrographia*.

STEPPING UP THE POWER
Under a modern low-power microscope, the spines of a nettle leaf can be clearly seen. The image is sharp because, like all modern microscopes, it has achromatic lenses (p. 17). These prevent colors from being dispersed.

1826 compound microscope with achromatic lenses

Eyepiece lens

Barrel

Objective lens

Focusing screw

Lens for focusing light on the specimen

Light rays from the specimen

Stage for holding specimen

Lens for illuminating specimen

Mirror reflecting light from lamp or window

Eye

How a compound microscope works

Eyepiece lens

Path of light as traced back by the eye

Magnified "real" image

Objective lens

Highly magnified "virtual" image

Specimen

Line showing midpoint of lenses

COMPOUND MICROSCOPES
At its simplest, a compound microscope needs just two lenses – a small but powerful objective lens, and a larger eyepiece lens. Light from the specimen is focused by the objective lens so that it forms a magnified "real" image (p. 12). The eyepiece lens then enlarges this just like a magnifying glass, so that the observer's eye traces the light back to see a much bigger "virtual" image. A two-lens microscope produces an image that is inverted, or back-to-front.

Nettle specimen

Network of veins

Hard spines on underside of leaf inject the nettle's poison

SHARING THE VIEW
This 19th-century microscope was designed to let up to four people look at the same specimen. There is just one objective lens, but the light from it is split with a prism so that it travels through four different eyepieces. Many modern microscopes use prisms to give a two-way "split." One group of light rays goes to the observer, and the other group of rays goes to a camera, which records the image on film.

Recording light

NEARLY A THOUSAND years ago the Arab scientist Alhazen (p. 18) explained how the sun's image could be produced in a darkened room. The light was made to pass through a small hole in one wall, so that it formed an image on a wall opposite. The *camera obscura*, which is Latin for "darkened room," became a popular curiosity used for seeing the sun and for looking at streets and landscapes. By the 1660s portable camera obscuras had been designed that had lenses, paper screens, and even focusing mechanisms. In fact, they had all the makings of modern cameras – except that they had no way to "record" the images that they formed. More than 150 years passed before Joseph Niepce discovered a method to record light, and true photography was born.

EARLIEST SURVIVING PHOTOGRAPH
In 1822 Joseph Niepce (1765-1833) focused this view from his window onto a sheet of pewter coated with light-sensitive bitumen. After eight hours he rinsed it with lavender oil and white petroleum. The bitumen washed away, except where light had fallen on it; the remaining bitumen made a photograph.

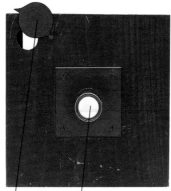

William Fox Talbot

Negatives and positives

Almost simultaneously, practical photography was invented by Willam Fox Talbot and Louis Daguerre, but Daguerre's method of making photographs is not the one that is in use today. Instead, modern cameras use the technique that was pioneered in the early 1830s by Talbot (1800-1877). He soaked paper in silver chloride, a chemical that darkens when exposed to light. When he let light fall on the paper, it produced a "negative" image. By using the same process to copy the negative, he could then make an unlimited number of "positive" prints.

Talbot's camera (front view)

Fixed-focus lens

Viewfinder with flap to shut off light

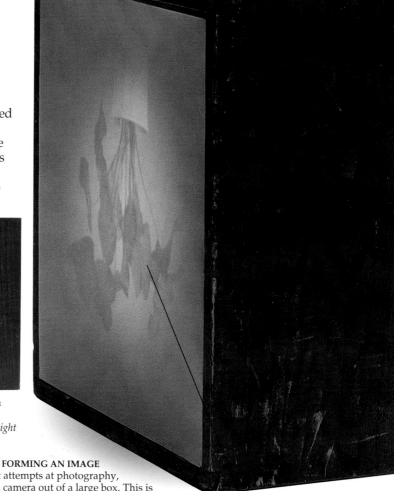

Using Fox Talbot's experimental camera of 1835

Upside-down image thrown on screen

PAPER NEGATIVE
William Fox Talbot made this tiny negative in August 1835. It shows a window of his home, Lacock Abbey, in England. The light-sensitive paper was exposed for half an hour.

FORMING AN IMAGE
During his first attempts at photography, William Fox Talbot made a camera out of a large box. This is an experimental version of one that he made in 1835. The box had a single lens, which created an upside-down image. Fox Talbot positioned light-sensitive paper at the back of the box and let some light fall on it for more than an hour. But the results were disappointing. Not enough light fell on the paper to expose it properly, so the image had very little detail. Talbot got around this problem by making much smaller cameras, just over 2 ½ in (6 cm) square. With these cameras the lens was very close to the paper, so the light falling on the paper was more intense. With one of these tiny cameras, Talbot made his famous negative shown on the left.

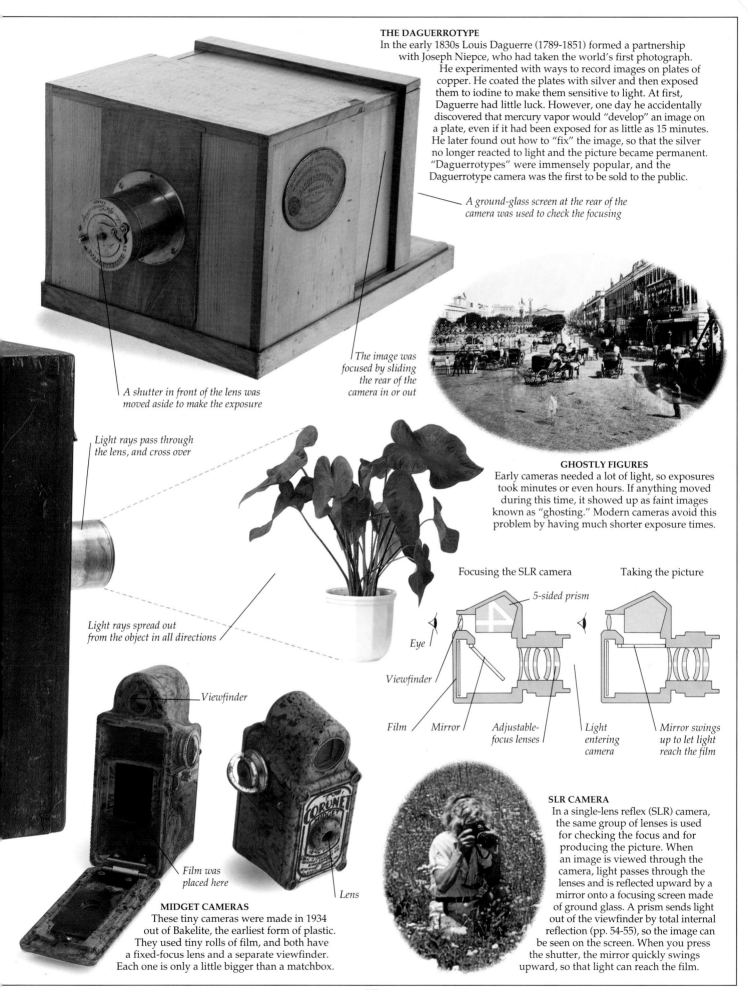

THE DAGUERROTYPE

In the early 1830s Louis Daguerre (1789-1851) formed a partnership with Joseph Niepce, who had taken the world's first photograph. He experimented with ways to record images on plates of copper. He coated the plates with silver and then exposed them to iodine to make them sensitive to light. At first, Daguerre had little luck. However, one day he accidentally discovered that mercury vapor would "develop" an image on a plate, even if it had been exposed for as little as 15 minutes. He later found out how to "fix" the image, so that the silver no longer reacted to light and the picture became permanent. "Daguerrotypes" were immensely popular, and the Daguerrotype camera was the first to be sold to the public.

A ground-glass screen at the rear of the camera was used to check the focusing

The image was focused by sliding the rear of the camera in or out

A shutter in front of the lens was moved aside to make the exposure

Light rays pass through the lens, and cross over

Light rays spread out from the object in all directions

GHOSTLY FIGURES

Early cameras needed a lot of light, so exposures took minutes or even hours. If anything moved during this time, it showed up as faint images known as "ghosting." Modern cameras avoid this problem by having much shorter exposure times.

Focusing the SLR camera

Taking the picture

5-sided prism

Eye

Viewfinder

Film   Mirror   Adjustable-focus lenses

Light entering camera

Mirror swings up to let light reach the film

Viewfinder

Film was placed here

Lens

MIDGET CAMERAS

These tiny cameras were made in 1934 out of Bakelite, the earliest form of plastic. They used tiny rolls of film, and both have a fixed-focus lens and a separate viewfinder. Each one is only a little bigger than a matchbox.

SLR CAMERA

In a single-lens reflex (SLR) camera, the same group of lenses is used for checking the focus and for producing the picture. When an image is viewed through the camera, light passes through the lenses and is reflected upward by a mirror onto a focusing screen made of ground glass. A prism sends light out of the viewfinder by total internal reflection (pp. 54-55), so the image can be seen on the screen. When you press the shutter, the mirror quickly swings upward, so that light can reach the film.

Projecting pictures

WHEN A PICTURE IS TAKEN with a camera (pp. 24-25) the lens gathers and focuses light to produce a small upside-down image on the film. Imagine what would happen if the film were replaced with a small light source. The light rays would then move in exactly the opposite direction. The same lens would produce a large image outside the camera that could be focused on a screen. The camera would now be a projector. Projectors produce still images, but if the images change very quickly – more than about 15 times a second – the eyes and brain cannot keep up with them. Instead of seeing lots of separate pictures, "persistence of vision" makes the pictures seem to merge together. When this happens only the changes within each still image (like an arm moving) are noticed. In the 1880s and 1890s a number of people, including the French brothers Auguste and Louis Lumière, used this principle to make moving pictures. They devised cameras that could take pictures in quick succession and projectors that could show them at the same speed. The result was the illusion of movement – or motion pictures.

MAGIC MOMENTS
During the 19th century "magic lantern" shows were a very popular form of entertainment, and they attracted large audiences. This lantern could make images that "dissolved" from one to another.

OIL-FIRED LANTERN
This "magic lantern" was built about 1895. It used a three-wick oil lamp to shine a powerful beam through glass slides. At the beginning of a lantern show, the projectionist would light the lamp and then push it into position at the back of the lantern. Inside, a concave mirror behind the lamp reflected the light forward, and this was bent inward by a set of condenser lenses so that it passed through the picture on the slide. The light then traveled through a projection lens, which could be moved backward or forward to focus an image on the screen. Once the show was under way, the lanternist had to be careful not to touch the top of the lantern, because it became very hot.

"New Pattern Helioscopic Lantern," c.1895, viewed from above

Focusing wheel for projection lens

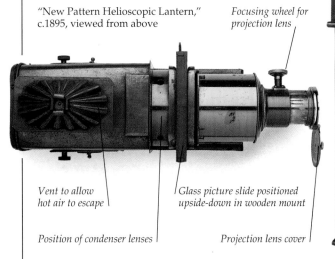

Vent to allow hot air to escape

Glass picture slide positioned upside-down in wooden mount

Position of condenser lenses

Projection lens cover

Control knobs to adjust the height of each wick

Viewing window for inspecting oil lamp

Walter Tyler's
NEW PATTERN
"HELIOSCOPIC LANTERN"
REGᵈ Nᵒ 73881
48₊50, WATERLOO ROAD,
LONDON S.E.

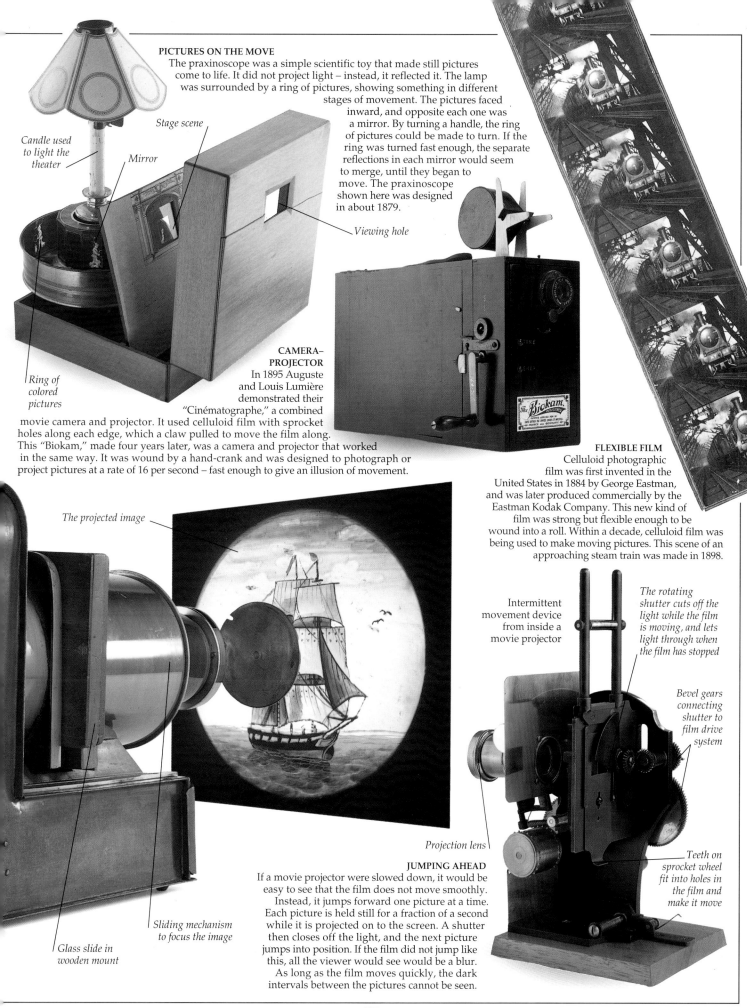

PICTURES ON THE MOVE

The praxinoscope was a simple scientific toy that made still pictures come to life. It did not project light – instead, it reflected it. The lamp was surrounded by a ring of pictures, showing something in different stages of movement. The pictures faced inward, and opposite each one was a mirror. By turning a handle, the ring of pictures could be made to turn. If the ring was turned fast enough, the separate reflections in each mirror would seem to merge, until they began to move. The praxinoscope shown here was designed in about 1879.

Candle used to light the theater

Stage scene

Mirror

Viewing hole

Ring of colored pictures

CAMERA–PROJECTOR

In 1895 Auguste and Louis Lumière demonstrated their "Cinématographe," a combined movie camera and projector. It used celluloid film with sprocket holes along each edge, which a claw pulled to move the film along. This "Biokam," made four years later, was a camera and projector that worked in the same way. It was wound by a hand-crank and was designed to photograph or project pictures at a rate of 16 per second – fast enough to give an illusion of movement.

FLEXIBLE FILM

Celluloid photographic film was first invented in the United States in 1884 by George Eastman, and was later produced commercially by the Eastman Kodak Company. This new kind of film was strong but flexible enough to be wound into a roll. Within a decade, celluloid film was being used to make moving pictures. This scene of an approaching steam train was made in 1898.

The projected image

Intermittent movement device from inside a movie projector

The rotating shutter cuts off the light while the film is moving, and lets light through when the film has stopped

Bevel gears connecting shutter to film drive system

Projection lens

Sliding mechanism to focus the image

Glass slide in wooden mount

Teeth on sprocket wheel fit into holes in the film and make it move

JUMPING AHEAD

If a movie projector were slowed down, it would be easy to see that the film does not move smoothly. Instead, it jumps forward one picture at a time. Each picture is held still for a fraction of a second while it is projected on to the screen. A shutter then closes off the light, and the next picture jumps into position. If the film did not jump like this, all the viewer would see would be a blur. As long as the film moves quickly, the dark intervals between the pictures cannot be seen.

Splitting light

In 1665 a great plague raged through Britain. The famous University of Cambridge was closed, but a young student named Isaac Newton continued his studies there and at home. This period of intense work was to turn him into the greatest figure that science had yet known. Newton experimented with a prism to see how it made light bend, and he noticed that a prism seemed to bend light of different colors by different amounts. He decided to investigate what happened when daylight passed through a prism and was thrown on to a screen. To begin with he worked with light shining through a round hole in his shutters. This produced a stretched image of the Sun, with a blue top edge and a red lower edge. But when the light went through a narrow slit before reaching the prism, the result was spectacular. Now, instead of mainly white light, he saw a multicolored band called a spectrum. Through this experiment and others, Newton concluded that white light is a mixture of many colors. His prism refracted, or bent, the colors by different amounts, making them spread out, or "disperse," so that they could be seen.

Newton let a beam of sunlight through a small hole in the shutter of his window

NEWTON'S PRISM EXPERIMENTS
"In a very dark Chamber, at a round hole . . . made in the Shut of a Window, I placed a glass Prism . . . ." So begins one chapter in Newton's *Opticks,* a book that describes his experiments with light and color. Newton did more than just split white light into a spectrum. He also combined it again, and he investigated the different colors that his prisms produced. In his crucial experiment (shown here), white light is split by one prism, so that it forms a spectrum. The spectrum falls on a screen with a small slit, so that light of just one color can pass through. This light then passes through another prism, which bends it by a particular angle but fails to split it into many colors. Newton learned from this that the colors were in the white light – they were not produced by the prism.

The first prism splits the light into a spectrum of colors

The spectrum fans out and meets a screen

ISAAC NEWTON

The work of Isaac Newton (1642-1727) dominated physics for nearly two centuries. He published two of the most important scientific books ever written: *Principia* (1687), which explained his laws of motion and theory of gravitation; and *Opticks* (1704), which investigated light. In 1703 he became President of the Royal Society, a distinguished scientific "club" formed in 1662. An independent, brilliant thinker, Newton was not an easy man to get along with.

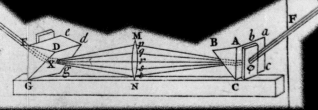

COMBINING AND SPLITTING
With this diagram (to be read from right to left) from *Opticks,* Newton described how a beam of sunlight could be split into colors, and then recombined to form white light once more. He did this by passing light ("O") through a prism and then a lens. The lens made the different colors converge on a second prism. This second prism spread the converging light rays so that they became parallel, forming a beam of white light. In this experiment, Newton used a third prism ("Y") to split the beam of white light again. This light was made to fall on a screen. He found that if he cut out or "intercepted" any of the colored light that hit the lens, this color would disappear from the spectrum on the screen.

SPARKLING GEMS
A cut diamond acts like a collection of prisms. When light passes through the diamond, the colors are dispersed and then reflected back out (p. 13). The angle of each facet, or side of the gem, is specially calculated to give the diamond its "fire."

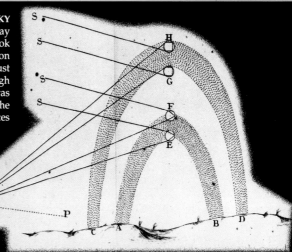

COLORS IN THE SKY
Newton wrote about the way rainbows are colored in his book *Opticks*. He knew that refraction (p. 14) was involved, and that it must occur when sunlight passes through raindrops. However, Newton was not the first to suggest this. The French philosopher René Descartes (p. 18) was the first person to reveal the mysteries of the rainbow. But as Newton's illustration shows, he was able to work out precisely how light from the Sun is split, and how it can form not just one rainbow, but sometimes two.

THE RAINBOW IN HISTORY
According to the Bible, the rainbow is a sign in the sky showing that the great flood will not be repeated. An old legend says that by digging at the foot of a rainbow, a pot of gold can be found. But however hard it is searched for, the foot can never be reached. This is because rainbows always move with the observer.

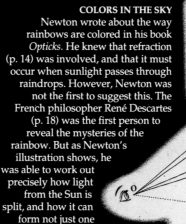

Red light is unchanged by passing through the prism

A narrow slit in the screen lets only light of a single color pass through

Red light passes through the slit

The red light meets a second prism, which refracts the light through an angle that can be measured

Red light that was not refracted because it "grazed," or did not pass through, the prism

DOUBLE BOWS
Rainbows are formed when sunlight shines through water droplets. The droplets reflect and refract the light rays, making their colors disperse into a spectrum. In a "primary" rainbow, colors are seen from light rays that enter each droplet from the top. In a "secondary" rainbow, colors are seen from rays entering droplets from the bottom. Secondary rainbows appear only when the sunlight is bright, and when the water droplets are uniformly spread out.

PRIMARY RAINBOW
In a primary rainbow white light is reflected just once as it travels through a raindrop. The colors are dispersed as they enter and leave the drop. The colors seen depend on the position of the drop in the sky. Red light is seen from raindrops at an angle of 42° to the line of the horizon, and blue light is seen from those at 40°. All other colors are seen from drops between these two angles.

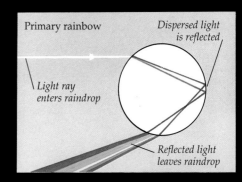

Primary rainbow

Dispersed light is reflected

Light ray enters raindrop

Reflected light leaves raindrop

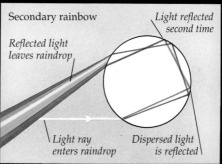

Secondary rainbow

Light reflected second time

Reflected light leaves raindrop

Light ray enters raindrop

Dispersed light is reflected

SECONDARY RAINBOW
A secondary rainbow forms outside a primary one. Light is reflected twice by each raindrop and emerges at a steeper angle to the ground. The order of the colors is reversed. (This is why a secondary rainbow seems like a reflection.) In a secondary rainbow, red light is seen from raindrops that are at an angle of 50° to the line of the horizon, and blue light from drops at an angle of 54°.

Adding light

W HEN A GREEN LIGHT AND A RED LIGHT are shone together on a wall, what color is seen? The answer isn't greenish-red or even reddish-green, but an entirely new color: yellow. If a third color – blue – is then added, the color changes again. Instead of greenish-reddish-blue, white light appears. When Isaac Newton conducted his splitting-light experiments (pp. 28-29), he made white light out of all the colors of the spectrum. But the experiment with colored lights on these two pages shows that the whole spectrum is not needed to make white light. In fact, just red, green, and blue can be added together to produce white. In various combinations, they will also make almost any other color. For this reason, they are known as the "additive primary colors."

SPINNING COLORS
This 19th-century spinning top was based on the same principle as Newton's color wheel (below). When the top spun, its colors added together, and one color was seen.

Red light

Blue light

When the wheel is still, the individual colors can be seen

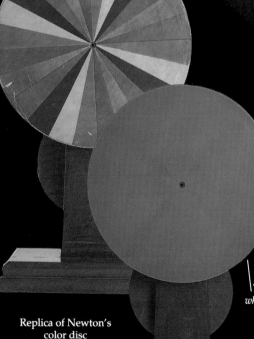

MIXING PRIMARIES
When spotlights of the primary colors – red, green, and blue – shine close together so that they overlap (right), the eyes receive a mixture of colors, which the brain interprets as one color. In the center the three colors mix to make white (this is pure only if the colors are balanced). Where two primary colors overlap, they produce a third color called a "secondary." There are three secondary colors: cyan (blue-green), yellow, and magenta.

The spinning wheel looks like one color

Replica of Newton's color disc

NEWTON'S COLOR DISC
Isaac Newton devised a special disc to show the principle of how colors mix together. This 19th-century replica is painted with a series of six different colors, repeated four times. If the wheel spins at more than about 100 revolutions a minute, the eye cannot keep track of the separate colors. Instead, the brain adds the six colors together to produce a new one – in this case, light brown.

PAINTING WITH DOTS
"Pointillism" is a style of painting, which was made famous by Impressionist artists such as Georges Seurat (1859-1891). Pointillists created their pictures by painting countless tiny dots of different colors. If a Pointillist painting is looked at closely, each individual colored dot can be seen. If viewed from farther away, the dots add together to give areas of a single color.

Green light

COLOR ON THE SCREEN
A color television picture is made up of tiny strips of red, green, and blue light. From the normal viewing distance, the colors from neighboring strips add together. The screen cannot produce pure colors such as yellow, but it can suggest yellow by lighting up neighboring green and red strips.

SEEING HIDDEN COLORS
A spectroscope is a device that disperses colors (p. 28) by bending them through different angles. Spectroscopes are used to show whether colors (reflected or created by an object) are pure or made by addition. The example below shows what would be seen when looking through a spectroscope at a red and a yellow pepper. The red pepper would give off red light only – red cannot be broken down into different colors. The yellow pepper would give off two hidden colors – green and red.

Red and blue mix together to produce magenta

Blue and green mix together to produce cyan

All three additive primary colors mix together to produce white

Red and green mix together to produce yellow

Only red light is reflected

Red and green are reflected and make yellow

Red pepper

Yellow pepper

Subtracting colors

ALL VISIBLE THINGS give off light, but they do it in two different ways. Some objects are light sources, meaning that they actually produce light. A flashlight, for example, produces light by using electrical energy to heat a filament (p. 52). If a flashlight is shone at a wall, the wall gives off light as well. But the wall is not a light source. It simply reflects light that has already been made. Things that do not produce light themselves are colored by a process called "color subtraction." When white light falls on them, they absorb some of its colors and reflect or transmit others. This is why a leaf, for example, looks green. It absorbs almost all the colors in sunlight except one – green – and reflects this, so green is the color that is seen. For thousands of years, people have sought substances that are particularly good at subtracting colors. They are used in pigments, dyes, paints, and inks. All of these substances make our world a more colorful place – not by making color, but by taking it away.

A flashlight ... using electrical energy to heat a filament (p. 52).

CAVE PAINTINGS
Cave paintings are the oldest surviving examples of human art. They were made with pigments that occur naturally in rocks, such as red ochre, and also with charcoal. Daylight makes most pigments fade over the years, but cave paintings are often deep inside the earth, so they have been well preserved. The painters would have worked by the flickering yellow light of burning torches.

Where the triangle and circle overlap, red and blue are removed, leaving green

Cyan

Where the triangle and square overlap, red and green are removed, leaving blue

Magenta

LEFTOVER COLORS
When the three primary colors of the spectrum are added together in pairs, they make three secondary colors (pp. 30-31). Here is shown what happens when the secondary colors – cyan, yellow, and magenta – are then illuminated by white light. On their own, each of the colored shapes takes away or "subtracts" just one primary color from white light. The color that is seen is formed because the brain adds together the colors that are left. Where two secondary colors overlap, two colors are subtracted, leaving a primary light color – red, green, or blue. In the middle, where the three shapes overlap, all three primary colors are taken away from white light. This leaves no colors at all – or black. White cannot be made by color subtraction. This is why colored paints or inks cannot be mixed to produce white.

MAKING MAGENTA
The square takes away green from white light, to leave red and blue, which the brain adds together to give magenta.

Where the circle and square overlap, blue and green are removed, leaving red

MAKING BLACK
Where all three shapes overlap, red, green, and blue are removed, leaving no light.

FOOD DYES

Today, many artificial substances are used to give food a brighter color than it really has. In days gone by, many food dyes were made from plants or from animals. Cochineal, a brilliant scarlet dye, was made from tiny insects that feed on a type of cactus. These insects were painstakingly gathered by hand and then squashed to make the dye.

A bottle of cochineal – a natural food dye

SCATTERING LIGHT

When white light is shone through a jar of water containing just a few drops of milk, blue light is scattered by the tiny particles in the water. Red light is not scattered, and instead passes through. This effect is called Rayleigh scattering. It makes the liquid glow, and gives it a blue tinge. Smoke sometimes has a bluish color caused by Rayleigh scattering from tiny particles of ash.

MAKING CYAN

The triangle takes away red from white light, leaving green and blue, which the brain adds together to give cyan.

THE CHANGING COLORS OF SUNLIGHT

The color of sunlight changes as it passes through the atmosphere because air takes away some colors more than others. This is clearly seen as the sun sinks at dusk. To begin with, the sun's light looks yellow. As it gets nearer to the horizon, its light has to travel sideways through a longer and longer slice of air, and it begins to turn orange and then red. This happens because the air absorbs more and more of the sun's blue light, leaving the longer red wavelengths (pp. 34-35).

Yellow

MAN-MADE DYES

In 1856 a young English chemist named William Perkin stumbled across an important discovery that started a giant industry. He was trying to make a drug called quinine out of chemicals prepared from coal tar. In one experiment, he accidentally produced a brilliantly colored substance which later came to be known as "mauveine." Perkin realized that mauveine had great potential as a dye. He set up a company to produce it, and made a fortune in the process. Today, nearly all dyes are man-made.

William Perkin
(1838-1907)

An original bottle of mauve dye

Shawl colored with William Perkin's mauve dye

A sample-book showing a range of colors produced by synthetic dyes

MAKING YELLOW

The circle takes away blue from white light, leaving red and green. The brain adds these to make yellow.

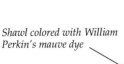

Particles and waves

It is easy enough to see the effects of light. But what is light made of, and how does it travel from one place to another? In the late 1600s Isaac Newton (p. 28) tried to answer these questions. He thought light could be made of particles or waves, and he did not want to rule either out. However, since the particle theory fitted most of the known phenomena and facts, it became popular with Newton's followers. The Dutch physicist Christian Huygens was not convinced by the particle theory. In 1690 he put forward a number of reasons for believing that light traveled in the form of waves. His evidence was strong, but over 100 years were to pass before an important experiment (p. 36) gave backing to the wave theory. In the early 1900s further discoveries were made (p. 44) about the nature of light. They showed that, in some ways, the followers of both Newton and Huygens were right.

The particles or waves of light bounce off the mirror, which then produces a reversed image of the candle

The flame produces particles or waves of light that radiate in all directions

MAKING SENSE OF LIGHT
Three of the most important characteristics of light are that it travels in straight lines, that it can be reflected, and that it can be bent when it passes from one medium to another. These two pages show how the two different ways of understanding light – the particle theory and the wave theory – explain each of these characteristics.

LIGHT AND WAVES
Christian Huygens (1629-1695) was a mathematician, physicist, and inventor who constructed the first pendulum clock and discovered the rings around the planet Saturn. In his book *Traité de la Lumiere*, published in 1690, he rejected the particle theory of light. He decided that because light moves so quickly it must be made up of waves rather than particles. Huygens suggested that light waves were carried by the "ether," an invisible, weightless substance that existed throughout air and space. In "Huygens's Principle," he showed that each point on a wave could be thought of as producing its own wavelets, which add together to form a wave-front. This idea neatly explains how refraction (p. 14) works. Because waves can cross each other, his theory also explains why light rays do not crash into each other when they meet.

Christian Huygens

Huygens's wave model

Light rays are transmitted in straight lines

Light wave spreads in all directions

Wavelets add to form a "wave-front"

Each point on the wave is the source of a new "wavelet"

MAKING WAVES
Long after the days of Huygens and Newton, the inventor and physicist Charles Wheatstone (1802-1875) made this model to show how light waves work. The white beads represent the "ether," a substance that was thought to carry light waves. The model showed that ether carried light by vibrating at right angles to the light waves. Huygens had believed that ether vibrated in the same direction as light, squashing and stretching as it carried the light waves. It is now believed that ether does not exist.

Ether

Ether

Wheatstone wave machine

WAVES AND REFLECTION

According to the wave theory, a light source gives off light waves which spread out in all directions. If any of the waves strike a mirror, they are reflected according to the angles from which they arrive. Reflection turns each wave back to front – this is why the image seen is reversed. This diagram shows what happens. The shape of the waves depends on the size of the light source and how far the waves have traveled. The wave-front from a small nearby light will be strongly curved because it is close to the light source. The wave-front from a distant light is less curved.

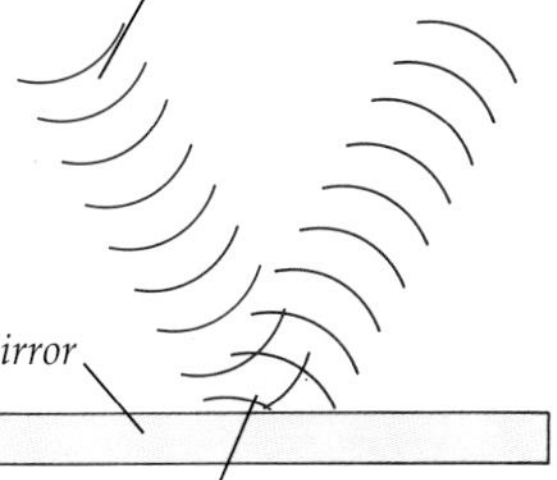

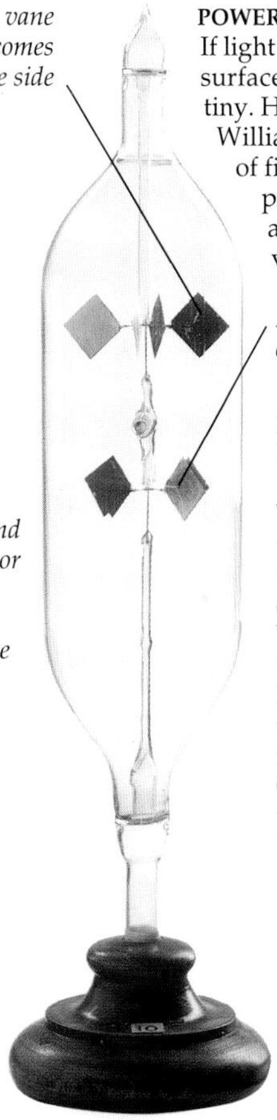

The dark side of each vane absorbs more light and becomes warmer than white side

Light waves

Mirror

Waves are reflected and reversed by the mirror

PARTICLES AND REFLECTION

According to the particle theory, reflection is very straightforward. Light arrives at a mirror as a stream of tiny particles, and these bounce off the mirror's surface. The particles are very small, so many of them travel side by side in a light ray. They bounce at different points, so their order is reversed by reflection, producing a reversed image. As with the wave theory, this kind of reflection would happen only with a smooth surface. If the surface was rough the particles would bounce at many different angles, so the light would be scattered.

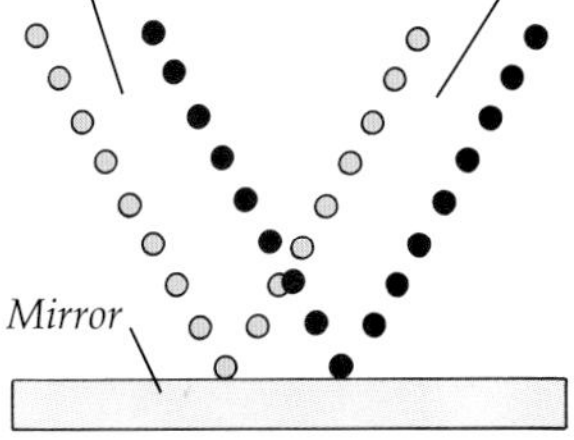

Light particles traveling toward the mirror from the foreground

Reflected, reversed particles travel away

Mirror

POWERED BY LIGHT

If light is made of particles, it should exert pressure when it hits a surface. Light does in fact do this, but the amount of pressure is tiny. How tiny can be seen with a radiometer, a device invented by William Crookes (1832-1919). In the radiometer light turns a set of finely balanced vanes. The glass bulb contains air at reduced pressure, and heated molecules of air bounce off the vanes and push them around. But if all the air is removed the vanes stop. Light pressure alone cannot push them around.

Air molecules collect heat energy from the dark side of vanes, bounce off the vanes, and push them around

PARTICLES AND SHADOWS

In his book *Opticks* of 1704, Isaac Newton wrote that "Light is never known to follow crooked Passages nor to bend into the Shadow." Newton explained this by saying that light particles always travel in straight lines. He thought that if an object stood in the path of the particles, it would cast a shadow because the particles could not spread out behind it. For everyday objects and their shadows, Newton was right. However, this idea did not agree with an important discovery made in 1665 by Francesco Grimaldi. Grimaldi found that on a very small scale, light could "bend into the shadow."

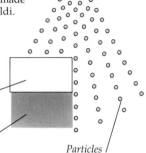

Light source

Object blocks some particles

On a large scale a shadow is cast in area where particles are blocked

Particles

WAVES AND SHADOWS

On a very small scale, shadows are not as simple as they seem. If light shines through a narrow slit (pp. 36-37) it spreads out, and the light beam becomes wider than might be expected. This effect is very difficult to explain by the particle theory of light, but it is easy with the wave theory. Water waves and sound waves spread out after passing through small gaps. If light is also a wave, it should be able to do the same thing.

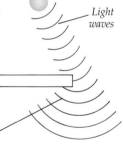

Light waves

Waves spreading out around a very small object

A shadow is formed by everyday objects when the waves or particles of light are blocked

Light waves or particles are refracted by the lens, producing a magnified image

WAVES AND REFRACTION

What happens when a beam of light hits a glass block at an angle? According to the wave theory, part of each advancing wave should meet the glass before the rest. This part will start to move through the glass, but it will travel more slowly than the part still in air. Because the same wave is traveling at two different speeds, the wave-front will bend into the glass. This fits the facts of refraction (p. 14).

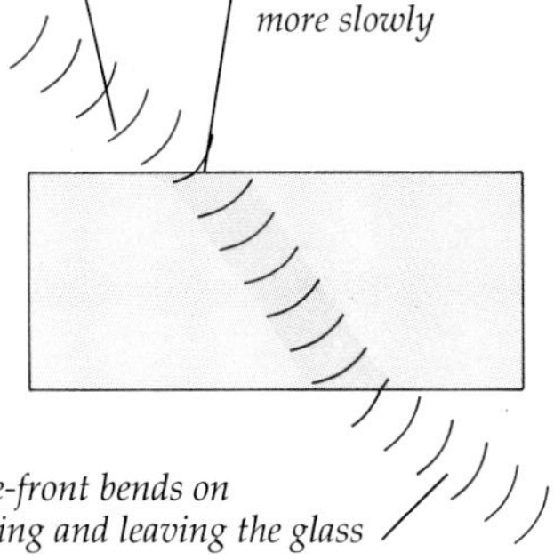

Rest of wave still in air

Edge of wave meets glass and travels more slowly

Wave-front bends on entering and leaving the glass

PARTICLES AND REFRACTION

Newton had difficulty explaining why particles of light should change course when they pass from air into glass. He thought that a special force might speed the particles as they entered the glass, and slow them down as they left it. He explained how refraction could disperse colors (p. 28) by suggesting that the rays of each color move in "fits." Each color had "fits" of a different length – an idea very much like wavelengths.

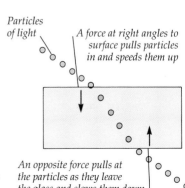

Particles of light

A force at right angles to surface pulls particles in and speeds them up

An opposite force pulls at the particles as they leave the glass and slows them down

Diffraction and interference

In 1801 AN ENGLISH PHYSICIST named Thomas Young described an experiment that led to a change in the understanding of light. Young had studied the eye and the human voice, and this made him think of similarities between light and sound. Many people believed that sound traveled in waves, and it seemed very likely to Young that light did as well. Like the Italian scientist Francesco Grimaldi, Young noticed that light rays spread out, or were "diffracted," when they passed through a very small slit. Young went on to see what happened when sunlight passed through two slits side by side, and then fell on a screen. He found that if the slits were large and far apart he saw two overlapping patches of light. But if the slits were very narrow and close together, the light produced bands of color, called "interference fringes." Young realized that these colored bands could be produced only by waves.

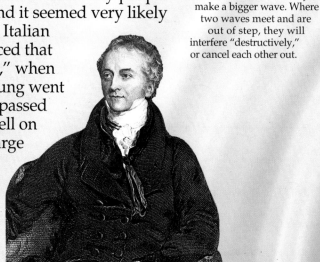

MAKING WAVES
Interference happens not only with light waves, but with sound and water waves, too. If the surface of a still pool of water is tapped with a thumb and forefinger, two sets of waves will be produced. Like light waves, they will spread out in all directions. Where two waves meet and are in step, they will interfere "constructively" to make a bigger wave. Where two waves meet and are out of step, they will interfere "destructively," or cancel each other out.

THOMAS YOUNG
Together with Auguste Fresnel (p. 17), Thomas Young (1773-1829) put together important evidence showing that light travels in waves. He concluded that different colors are made of waves of different lengths. Young carried out his experiments with great care, but his conclusions were not immediately accepted. During the 18th century it was believed that light was made of particles, and people were slow to change their views.

MAKING LIGHT DIFFRACT *(left)*
A diffraction grating, like the one at the upper left of this picture, is a small glass slide engraved with many narrow slits, through which light is made to pass. The spreading light waves interfere with each other to produce streaks of color. In a typical diffraction grating, there are about 7,500 per inch (about 3,000 lines per cm), carefully positioned so that they are all exactly the same distance apart.

HOW INTERFERENCE WORKS
In Thomas Young's experiment, light shines through one narrow slit cut into a screen, which makes the light spread out, or "diffract." It then reaches a screen with two more narrow slits, which are very close together. This creates two sources of light, which diffract once more. As the light waves from each slit spread out, they meet each other. Sometimes the waves will be exactly in step, and sometimes they will be slightly or completely out of step. If the waves are in step they will add together – this is called constructive interference. If the waves are out of step they will cancel each other out – this is known as destructive interference. The effect of the two kinds of interference can be seen because they make bright or dark "fringes" where the light hits the screen. Interference is produced by anything that splits light into waves that can be added together or cancelled out. Diffraction gratings, bubbles, compact discs, and even butterfly wings (pp. 38-39) all create interference patterns.

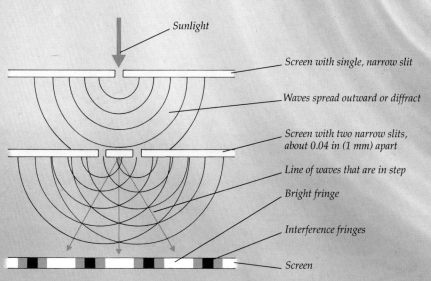

Sunlight

Screen with single, narrow slit

Waves spread outward or diffract

Screen with two narrow slits, about 0.04 in (1 mm) apart

Line of waves that are in step

Bright fringe

Interference fringes

Screen

The thumb and forefinger act like two light sources, producing waves of the same length that radiate outward

Where two waves meet and are exactly out of step, they interfere destructively, and the water stays level

Where the waves meet and are exactly in step, they interfere constructively to make a higher peak or a deeper trough

BENDING AROUND CORNERS

In everyday circumstances light seems to travel in straight lines. But in 1665 Francesco Grimaldi noticed that light seemed to bend and spread out when it passed through a narrow slit. He called this bending "diffraction." Today, microscopes and camera lenses are powerful enough to show how light is diffracted by sharp edges. This photograph, taken through a special filter, shows how light bends around the sharp edges of a metal bolt, giving it a fuzzy outline.

BARTON'S BUTTONS

These metal buttons were made by John Barton in about 1830. Each one has a pattern of fine lines scratched on its surface. The lines work like a diffraction grating. They reflect bright sunlight so that neighboring waves interfere with each other.

Interference in action

INTERFERENCE IS SOMETHING that can be seen not only in optical experiments, but in many different objects – living and nonliving. It makes up some of the most brilliant colors and intricate patterns in the world. Interference colors are created in a different way from colors that are produced by pigments (pp. 32-33). In daylight, a pigmented surface – like a piece of blue paper – always looks the same, no matter how it is seen. But if you look at a film of oil floating on water, or at a peacock's tail feather, things are different. The colors you see will depend on the angle from which you look. If you move your head, the colors will change, and may disappear altogether. This happens because these "iridescent" colors are produced by the shape of separate surfaces that are a tiny distance apart. The surfaces reflect light in a special way, making the light rays interfere with one another.

IRIDESCENT OPAL
Opal is made up of microscopic silicate spheres stacked in regular layers. Each sphere reflects light, and the reflected light rays interfere to produce brilliant colors. Turning the opal changes the colors that are seen.

NEWTON'S RINGS
When a convex lens is placed on a flat glass plate, light is reflected by the plate and by the lower surface of the lens. The two groups of rays interfere with each other to produce "Newton's Rings." These are named after Isaac Newton (1642-1727), who first investigated the effect.

Interference creates colorful patterns

BRIGHT EYES
The "eyes" in these peacock feathers are colored by tiny rods of a substance called melanin. The rods are arranged in a way that produces interference when light falls on them.

INSIDE A SHELL
The beautiful silvery colors inside this abalone shell are brought about by very thin layers of nacre – a hard mineral. Each layer reflects light, and the reflected rays interfere with each other to create colors. The metallic colors of some beetles are produced in the same way, by thin layers of a substance called chitin (pronounced *kytin*).

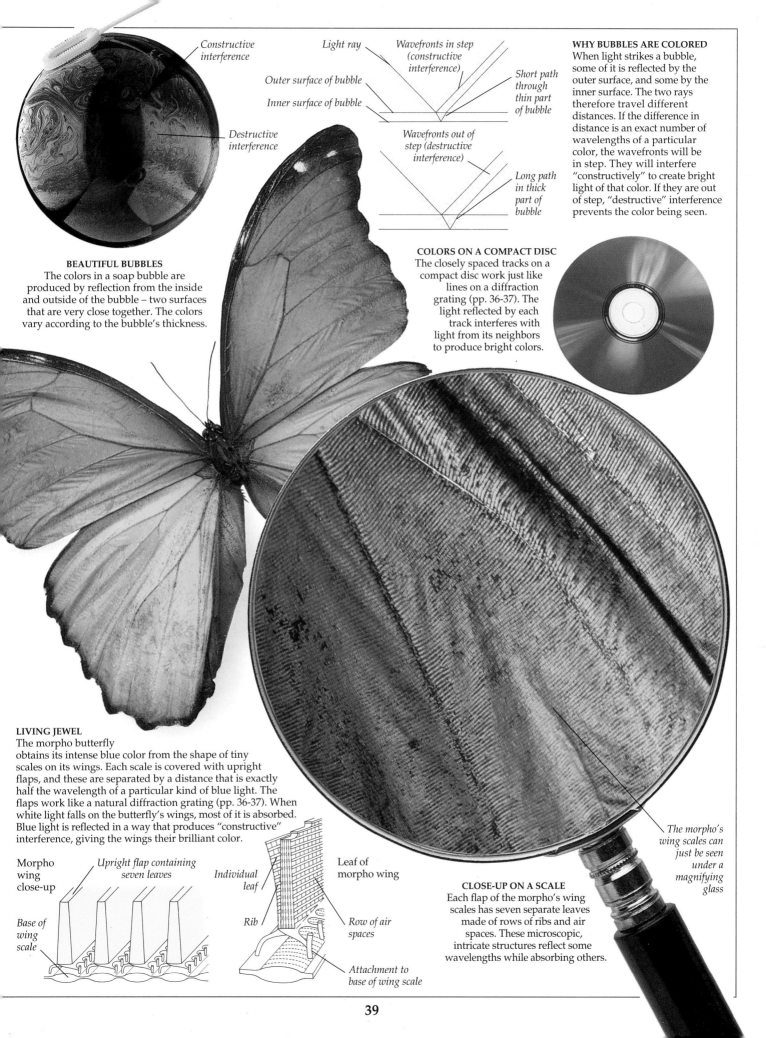

Constructive interference

Destructive interference

BEAUTIFUL BUBBLES
The colors in a soap bubble are produced by reflection from the inside and outside of the bubble – two surfaces that are very close together. The colors vary according to the bubble's thickness.

Light ray

Wavefronts in step (constructive interference)

Outer surface of bubble

Inner surface of bubble

Short path through thin part of bubble

Wavefronts out of step (destructive interference)

Long path in thick part of bubble

WHY BUBBLES ARE COLORED
When light strikes a bubble, some of it is reflected by the outer surface, and some by the inner surface. The two rays therefore travel different distances. If the difference in distance is an exact number of wavelengths of a particular color, the wavefronts will be in step. They will interfere "constructively" to create bright light of that color. If they are out of step, "destructive" interference prevents the color being seen.

COLORS ON A COMPACT DISC
The closely spaced tracks on a compact disc work just like lines on a diffraction grating (pp. 36-37). The light reflected by each track interferes with light from its neighbors to produce bright colors.

LIVING JEWEL
The morpho butterfly obtains its intense blue color from the shape of tiny scales on its wings. Each scale is covered with upright flaps, and these are separated by a distance that is exactly half the wavelength of a particular kind of blue light. The flaps work like a natural diffraction grating (pp. 36-37). When white light falls on the butterfly's wings, most of it is absorbed. Blue light is reflected in a way that produces "constructive" interference, giving the wings their brilliant color.

Morpho wing close-up

Upright flap containing seven leaves

Individual leaf

Rib

Base of wing scale

Leaf of morpho wing

Row of air spaces

Attachment to base of wing scale

CLOSE-UP ON A SCALE
Each flap of the morpho's wing scales has seven separate leaves made of rows of ribs and air spaces. These microscopic, intricate structures reflect some wavelengths while absorbing others.

The morpho's wing scales can just be seen under a magnifying glass

The electromagnetic spectrum

IN 1799 AND 1800 William Herschel set up dozens of different experiments to test the link between light and heat. In one he formed a spectrum with a prism and then screened out all but one of the colors. He let this light fall on a thermometer and recorded the temperature that it showed. Herschel found that violet light gave the lowest reading on the thermometer. Red gave a higher reading, but the highest reading of all was produced beyond the red end of the spectrum, where there was no light to be seen. He had discovered "infrared" radiation – a form of wave energy that can be felt, but not seen by human eyes. Herschel decided that light and infrared rays were two quite different forms of energy. However, other scientists, including Thomas Young (p. 36), thought that they were similar. Today it is known that both light waves and infrared waves are part of a wide spectrum of wave energy – the "electromagnetic spectrum." Humans can see light because the eyes contain special nerve endings that are sensitive to a particular range of wavelengths. The rest of the electromagnetic spectrum is invisible to humans.

HEAT AND THE SPECTRUM
In this experiment Herschel tested the heating power of each color of the spectrum. He split light with a prism, and the spectrum fell onto a screen with a slit cut in it. Light of one color passed through the slit and fell on a thermometer. He also performed experiments to see if "invisible light" (infra-red) could be refracted, and found that it could.

WILLIAM HERSCHEL
Originally a musician, William Herschel (1738-1822) became a prominent figure in the history of astronomy. He played an important part in the development of the reflecting telescope (pp. 20-21), using mirrors that he cast and polished himself. In 1781 he discovered the planet Uranus.

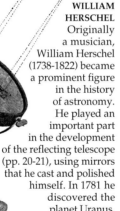

BEYOND THE VISIBLE
William Herschel investigated the link between light and heat in order to solve a practical problem. He wanted to look at sunspots through his telescope, but he found that even with colored filters the sun's heat was too great for comfortable viewing. He thought that if he could find out exactly which colors were "more apt to occasion heat" he could do something to cut them out. His experiments helped him devise green lenses which blocked some of the heat.

THREE-COLOR VISION
Isaac Newton (p. 28) showed that sunlight is made of a spectrum of different colors. Each color merges gradually into its neighbors to give different "hues." Most people can see about five main colors in the spectrum, but the number of hues is almost limitless. So how do the eyes distinguish among them? In 1801 Thomas Young (p. 36) suggested that the eye has three types of color receptor, and that the mix of signals that they produce tells what kind of light is being seen. Young's idea of "trichromacy" was correct. The eyes have three types of nerve endings, or "cones," for colored light. Each type of cone is most sensitive to a different range of colors. If violet light is seen, only one type of cone produces a signal, which the brain interprets as "violet." With an equal mixture of red, green, and blue light, signals are produced by all types of cone. The brain interprets this as "white."

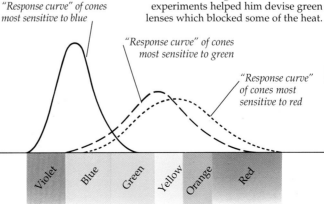

"Response curve" of cones most sensitive to blue

"Response curve" of cones most sensitive to green

"Response curve" of cones most sensitive to red

Violet Blue Green Yellow Orange Red

Response of cones to light
(measured by light absorption of each of the three types of cone)

Thermometer placed outside the visible spectrum is heated by invisible infrared light, which produces more heating than visible red light

Thermometer heated by visible red light

The visible spectrum

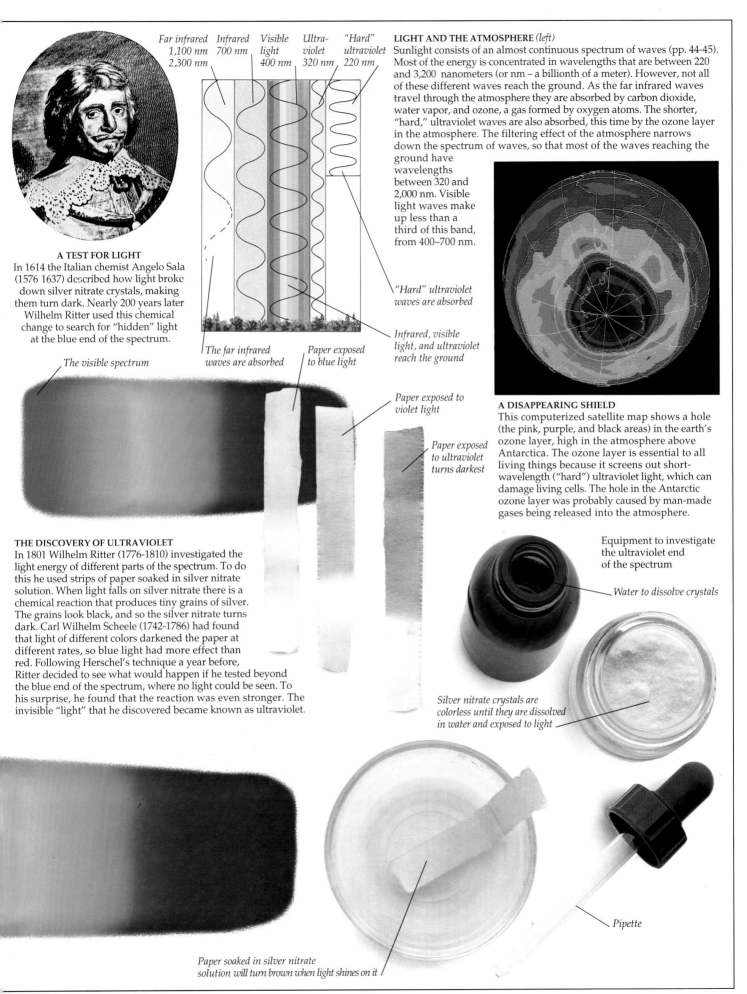

Far infrared 1,100 nm 2,300 nm
Infrared 700 nm
Visible light 400 nm
Ultra-violet 320 nm
"Hard" ultraviolet 220 nm

A TEST FOR LIGHT

In 1614 the Italian chemist Angelo Sala (1576 1637) described how light broke down silver nitrate crystals, making them turn dark. Nearly 200 years later Wilhelm Ritter used this chemical change to search for "hidden" light at the blue end of the spectrum.

The far infrared waves are absorbed

The visible spectrum

Paper exposed to blue light

Paper exposed to violet light

Paper exposed to ultraviolet turns darkest

Infrared, visible light, and ultraviolet reach the ground

"Hard" ultraviolet waves are absorbed

LIGHT AND THE ATMOSPHERE (left)

Sunlight consists of an almost continuous spectrum of waves (pp. 44-45). Most of the energy is concentrated in wavelengths that are between 220 and 3,200 nanometers (or nm – a billionth of a meter). However, not all of these different waves reach the ground. As the far infrared waves travel through the atmosphere they are absorbed by carbon dioxide, water vapor, and ozone, a gas formed by oxygen atoms. The shorter, "hard," ultraviolet waves are also absorbed, this time by the ozone layer in the atmosphere. The filtering effect of the atmosphere narrows down the spectrum of waves, so that most of the waves reaching the ground have wavelengths between 320 and 2,000 nm. Visible light waves make up less than a third of this band, from 400–700 nm.

A DISAPPEARING SHIELD

This computerized satellite map shows a hole (the pink, purple, and black areas) in the earth's ozone layer, high in the atmosphere above Antarctica. The ozone layer is essential to all living things because it screens out short-wavelength ("hard") ultraviolet light, which can damage living cells. The hole in the Antarctic ozone layer was probably caused by man-made gases being released into the atmosphere.

THE DISCOVERY OF ULTRAVIOLET

In 1801 Wilhelm Ritter (1776-1810) investigated the light energy of different parts of the spectrum. To do this he used strips of paper soaked in silver nitrate solution. When light falls on silver nitrate there is a chemical reaction that produces tiny grains of silver. The grains look black, and so the silver nitrate turns dark. Carl Wilhelm Scheele (1742-1786) had found that light of different colors darkened the paper at different rates, so blue light had more effect than red. Following Herschel's technique a year before, Ritter decided to see what would happen if he tested beyond the blue end of the spectrum, where no light could be seen. To his surprise, he found that the reaction was even stronger. The invisible "light" that he discovered became known as ultraviolet.

Equipment to investigate the ultraviolet end of the spectrum

Water to dissolve crystals

Silver nitrate crystals are colorless until they are dissolved in water and exposed to light

Pipette

Paper soaked in silver nitrate solution will turn brown when light shines on it

Electromagnetic waves

After William Herschel discovered the existence of infrared light beyond the red end of the visible spectrum (pp. 40-41), the Danish physicist Hans Christian Oersted (1777-1851) found that an electric current could make the needle of a compass change direction. In the same year the French scientist André-Marie Ampère (1775-1836) showed that two wires that were carrying electric currents could be made to attract or repel each other, just like magnets. More experiments followed thick and fast, and it became clear that electricity and magnetism were somehow linked. In 1865 the Scottish scientist James Clerk Maxwell used mathematics to explain the links between the two. He showed that electricity and magnetism are bound together so closely that they often act together as "electromagnetism." Maxwell realized that if an electric current was made to surge backward and forward, it would set up changing electromagnetic waves that would radiate outward at an immense speed. His calculations showed that these electromagnetic waves radiated at the speed of light (pp. 60-61). From this, Maxwell concluded that light itself was a form of electromagnetic wave.

CHANGING WAVES
Why do things glow when they are very hot? The answer is that they emit visible electromagnetic waves – or light. Even a very cold object, such as a block of ice, emits waves, but the waves are weak, and they are much too long for human eyes to detect. As an object becomes warmer, its atoms emit much more wave energy, and the waves it produces become shorter and shorter. If it is warmed enough, it will eventually start to glow. This happens because the waves it emits are now short enough for human eyes to see.

Heated atoms emit light at the red end of the visible spectrum

Cooler atoms give off longer infrared waves, which are invisible

1 BECOMING VISIBLE
A cold steel bar emits no visible light. It can be seen in daylight because it reflects light that falls on it. In the dark it is invisible. But if the bar is heated, it produces visible light. This bar is emitting light with wavelengths of about 700 nm – just within the red end of the visible spectrum.

TELEVISION
Television sound and pictures are carried on short-wavelength radio waves of less than 3.3 ft (1 m). The frequencies of the waves are modulated, to make them carry a signal.

Television Typical wavelength: 1.65 ft (0.5 m)

Radio waves Typical wavelength: 328 ft (100 m)

Radar Typical wavelength: 0.03 ft (0.01 m)

A SPECTRUM OF WAVELENGTHS *(right)*
Electromagnetic radiation makes up a whole spectrum of waves of many lengths. Red light, for example, has a wavelength of about 650 nm (a nanometer is a billionth of a meter). Another way of describing red light is to say that it has a "frequency" of 450 billion billion cycles, this being the number of waves of red light that will pass any point in one second. Radio waves have much longer wavelengths. Long-wave radio uses waves of up to 6,562 feet (2,000 meters) long – three billion times longer than red light waves.

JAMES CLERK MAXWELL
Scotsman James Clerk Maxwell (1831-1879) was a gifted mathematician who made key discoveries in many different areas of physics. One of his first achievements was the "Kinetic Theory of Gases," a mathematical investigation showing how the temperature of a gas is linked to the overall movement of its atoms or molecules. Maxwell used the same mathematical skills to produce equations describing how electricity and magnetism are linked. He was also interested in mechanics and astronomy, and in 1861 he made the world's first color photograph.

RADIO WAVES *(left)*
Radio waves range from about 1 mm to several miles in length. Radars, microwave ovens, televisions, and radios work by using different bands of radio waves. Radio waves are also produced by many stars and galaxies and can be detected by special telescopes. These radiotelescopes in New Mexico work together to gather waves from very distant objects.

RADAR *(below)*
A radar scanner emits very short radio waves and detects echoes from objects in their path. Radar is short for "Radio Detection and Ranging."

Cold atoms emit no visible light

Cooler atoms produce red light

Cooler areas on the surface absorb yellow light, so they look darker

The hottest atoms emit yellowish-white light

The hottest atoms emit orange light

The hottest atoms emit yellow light

3 YELLOW HEAT
The bar is now extremely hot. The most prominent color of light being emitted is yellow, with a wavelength of about 580 nm, though others are present. The hottest parts of the bar still emit orange and red light, but these colors are masked by the much more intense waves of yellow light.

4 WHITE HEAT
The heat is now so intense that the bar is radiating most colors of the visible spectrum, which add together (p. 30) to appear white.

2 ORANGE HEAT
The bar is now hotter still, and it is emitting more light. At this temperature more of the light emitted has a shorter wavelength – about 630 nm – giving the bar an orange color. Farther away from the tip of the bar the color changes because the temperature gradually decreases.

X-RAYS (*right*)
These rays (or waves) carry more energy than visible light. They are able to penetrate the soft parts of our bodies, but they cannot pass through bone. X-rays can be detected by photographic film, so they are used to produce pictures of things that cannot normally be seen, like broken bones.

COSMIC RAYS
The highest-energy radiation that exists is in cosmic rays. They contain tiny particles of atomic nuclei, as well as some electrons and gamma rays. Cosmic radiation bombards the earth's atmosphere from remote regions of space.

MICROWAVES
Low-level microwave radiation permeates space. It is thought to have been released by the "Big Bang" that may have created the universe. In a microwave oven, microwaves rapidly change the alignment of water molecules, and this heats up the food.

Visible light
Typical wavelength: 0.000,001,5 ft (0.000,000,5 m)

X-rays
Typical wavelength: 0.000,000,000,03 ft (0.000,000,000,01 m)

Cosmic rays
Typical wavelength: 0.000,000,000,000,03 ft (0.000,000,000,000,01 m)

Microwaves
Typical wavelength: 0.003–0.328 ft (.001–0.1 m)

Infrared waves
Typical wavelength: 0.000,164 ft (0.000,05 m)

Ultraviolet waves
Typical wavelength: 0.000,000,3 ft (0.000,000,1 m)

Gamma rays
Typical wavelength: 0.000,000,000,000,3 ft (0.000,000,000,000,1 m)

INFRARED WAVES (*below*)
Infrared waves are produced by things that are hot. In this satellite photograph of an erupting volcano, invisible infrared waves from molten lava have been processed by computer to make them a visible red color.

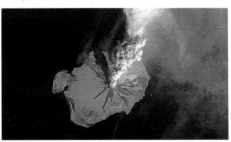

ULTRAVIOLET WAVES
Ultraviolet waves have lengths as short as 50 nm. They are produced by very hot objects, like the sun and other stars. Ultraviolet waves carry more energy than light waves, which is why they can penetrate and burn the skin. Some suntan lotions screen out the harmful ultraviolet light rays, and this prevents the skin from becoming damaged.

GAMMA RAYS (*left*)
Gamma rays (or waves), a form of radioactivity released by some atomic nuclei, have very short wavelengths. They carry a large amount of energy and can penetrate metals and concrete. They are very dangerous and can kill living cells, especially at the high levels released by nuclear reactions such as the explosion of a nuclear bomb.

Atoms and light

In 1802 WILLIAM HYDE WOLLASTON made a surprising discovery about light from the sun. He found that the sun's spectrum was not a continuous band of light. Instead, it contained hundreds of narrow lines where particular wavelengths were missing. A German physicist named Joseph von Fraunhofer mapped over 500 of these, giving the main ones letters. In the late 1850s a physicist named Gustav Kirchoff found that all atoms can emit or absorb particular wavelengths of light, and that the gaps in the Sun's spectrum were caused by absorption. This was a major discovery, because it showed that there were strong links between atoms and light. As the 20th century began, an important new theory emerged that explained how atoms and light interact.

The sun produces light

The lens focuses the sunlight on to a prism

The prism then splits the sunlight into a spectrum of colors

EVIDENCE FROM ELECTRONS

It was known in the 19th century that light had an effect on some metals – it could dislodge electrons from the atoms (electrons are the tiny particles in atoms that form electric currents). This phenomenon, which became known as the photoelectric effect, was investigated further in 1902 by the German physicist Philipp Lenard. Using a prism arranged like the one shown here, he and other physicists looked at the links between the wavelength of light, the release of electrons, and the energy that they had. The results were strange. For a given wavelength of light, the electrons had a fixed amount of energy. Weak light produced fewer electrons, but each electron still had just as much energy as if the light had been bright. However, there was a link between wavelength and energy. The shorter the wavelength of light, the more energy the electrons had. These findings were not understood until 1905, when Albert Einstein (p. 63) used "quantum theory" to solve the problem.

FRAUNHOFER LINES
In 1814 Joseph von Fraunhofer (1787-1826) plotted the sun's spectrum, now called Fraunhofer lines.

The number and the energy of the electrons is measured

Max Planck

A color is singled out with a lens to test its effect in dislodging electrons

The colored light is focused on to a metal plate

Observer looks at spectrum through tube containing lenses

THE QUANTUM THEORY

During the late 19th century physicists thought that light and other forms of electromagnetic radiation were continuous streams of energy. However, by 1900 this idea had led to a number of theoretical problems. Max Planck (1858-1947) tackled them by suggesting that the energy in radiation was not continuous, but that it was divided into tiny packets, or "quanta." His quantum theory showed that in some circumstances light could be thought of as particles, as believed by the followers of Issac Newton's particle theory (pp. 34-35).

EXAMINING A SPECTRUM
A spectrometer is a device used to investigate the light in a spectrum. This one was built in about 1905. The substance to be examined is placed in one tube, and white light shining through it is split by a diffraction grating (p. 36) on the central plinth. The observer looks at the spectrum through the other tube.

HOW ATOMS MAKE LIGHT

Why is light energy is produced in small packets, or "quanta"? The answer lies in the structure of atoms, the tiny particles that make up matter. An atom consists of a small and dense nucleus, surrounded by electrons – the same particles that produce electric currents. Electrons circle the nucleus at different distances. The farther they are from the nucleus, the more energy they have. If an electron moves from an outer orbit to one that is closer to the nucleus, it loses energy. This energy is released as a quantum of light, or photon. In most atoms, there are many electrons and many different energy levels. The wavelengths of light that each electron can produce depend on how much energy the electron loses in falling from one orbit to another. Together, these different wavelengths give an atom its characteristic "emission spectrum." By examining an emission spectrum, scientists can identify the kind of atom that produced it.

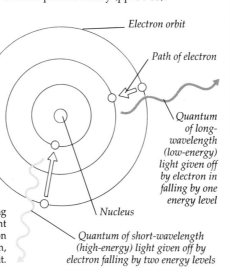

Electron orbit

Path of electron

Quantum of long-wavelength (low-energy) light given off by electron in falling by one energy level

Nucleus

Quantum of short-wavelength (high-energy) light given off by electron falling by two energy levels

LINES IN THE SPECTRUM
The strips above show the sun's spectrum in great detail. In it, hundreds of tiny lines called "Fraunhofer lines" can be seen. The sun's light is created by hot atoms on its surface. When this light travels through cooler atoms in the sun's outer atmosphere, some of its wavelengths are absorbed. Each kind of atom absorbs particular wavelengths, producing characteristic lines. Together they create an "absorption spectrum."

Fluorescence

Sometimes atoms absorb light of one wavelength, but almost immediately release the energy as light of another wavelength. This is called fluorescence. Fluorescence happens when an electron takes in energy and moves to a higher orbit, but then falls back to a lower orbit in a series of steps. Many substances fluoresce when ultraviolet light strikes them. We cannot see ultraviolet, but we can see the lower-energy light that fluorescence produces.

SOAP POWDER IN DAYLIGHT
In daylight soap powder looks bright and white. Some of this brightness is due to fluorescence.

WILLEMITE IN DAYLIGHT
Willemite is a mineral containing zinc and manganese. In daylight it looks brownish (the white is quartz).

SODALITE IN DAYLIGHT
This grayish mineral is a complex compound of sodium, aluminum, silicon, oxygen, and chlorine.

SOAP POWDER IN ULTRAVIOLET LIGHT
In ultraviolet light soap powder is intensely white. Fluorescence helps make clothes look clean.

WILLEMITE IN ULTRAVIOLET LIGHT
When willemite fluoresces, it emits a bright green light (the pink fluorescence is produced by quartz).

LIVING LIGHTS
These specks of light on the surface of the sea are created by luminescence in tiny plants and animals. They make light through a chemical reaction in which a protein combines with oxygen. The reaction produces light, but hardly any heat.

The diffraction grating splits the light from the substance to form a spectrum

SODALITE IN ULTRAVIOLET LIGHT
Sodalite absorbs ultraviolet light, and emits yellow or orange light.

Substance to be examined is placed in this tube and illuminated by a strong white light

SPECTRAL SAMPLES
Spectroscopy – the scientific study of spectra – began in the 1860s. These glass tubes were made in 1871 and contain solutions of different substances. They were used as a set of standards when examining spectra. Each of these substances absorbed particular wavelengths when light passed through it.

ULTRAVIOLET SPECTRUM
This photographic slide, made in about 1900, shows Fraunhofer lines of part of the "absorption spectra" of aluminum and hydrogen atoms. The atoms were illuminated with ultraviolet light, which was split into a spectrum to show which wavelengths were absorbed.

Letting light through

Translucent
comb

ABOUT 5,000 YEARS AGO, the Egyptians learned how to make glass. To begin with they shaped it into beads, but by Roman times glass was being "blown" to make cups and dishes as well. Glass became highly prized. Although it broke easily, it was almost transparent, and by comparison it made pottery look dull and uninteresting. Today, transparent objects – from plastic windows to glass bottles – are common, and they play an important part in day-to-day life. They let light through without scattering its rays. As a result, images can be seen through them clearly. Translucent objects also let light through, but scatter its rays. Because of this scattering, images behind a translucent object cannot be seen clearly. Opaque objects do not let any light through. They block light waves, though they may be transparent to other kinds of waves – X-rays, for example.

SEEING THE LIGHT
If a few drops of oil are added to a sheet of paper, the paper lets more light pass through.

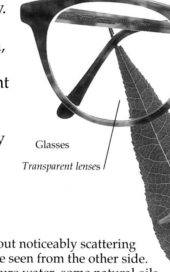

*Translucent
frame*

Glasses

Transparent lenses

Translucent
flower petals

Translucent
leaf

Transparency

Transparent objects let light pass through without noticeably scattering its rays. As a result, a clear image can usually be seen from the other side. Transparent materials are common in nature. Pure water, some natural oils, and the crystals of many minerals are transparent. But apart from a vacuum, nothing is ever completely see-through. Some light energy is always absorbed by the material that it passes through. The thicker something is, the more energy it will absorb. This is why things look clear through a thin layer of glass, but dull through a thick block.

Transparent molten wax

SEE-THROUGH FISH
This fish's body contains transparent oils that make it harder to see. This helps many small water animals to hide from their enemies.

Metal oxides in the glass subtract colors from white light

Transparent
quartz crystal

Transparent
glass

Translucent
bottle

Translucent
bottle

Translucent
bottle

Translucency

A translucent object lets some light through, but it scatters the rays so much that whatever is on the other side cannot be seen clearly. Many plastics, oils, fats, and waxes are translucent, as are thin layers of cells in plants and animals. Just like transparency, translucency depends on thickness. If a single sheet of paper is held up to a lamp, the fibers in the paper will scatter and absorb light, but some light will still pass through. If more and more sheets are gradually added to make a thicker layer, the light will eventually disappear. With some substances, translucency depends on temperature. Many fats and waxes scatter light less when they are liquid than when they are solid. This is why candlewax becomes see-through when it melts, and why butter becomes clear when it is warmed in a pan.

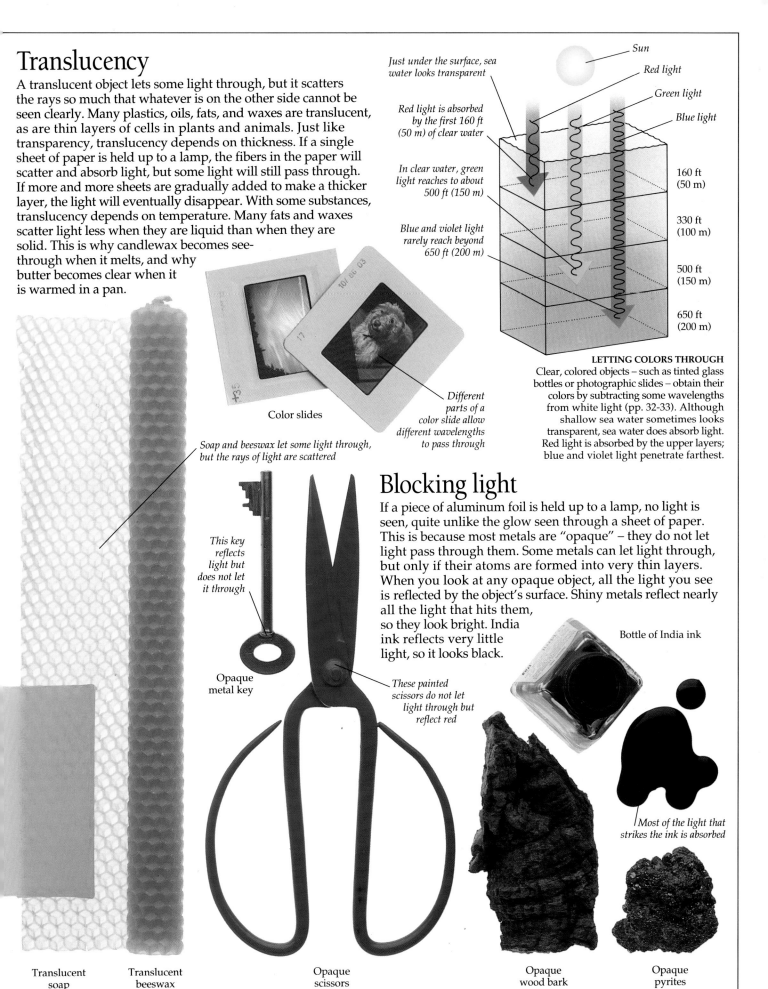

Just under the surface, sea water looks transparent

Sun

Red light

Green light

Blue light

Red light is absorbed by the first 160 ft (50 m) of clear water

In clear water, green light reaches to about 500 ft (150 m)

Blue and violet light rarely reach beyond 650 ft (200 m)

160 ft (50 m)

330 ft (100 m)

500 ft (150 m)

650 ft (200 m)

LETTING COLORS THROUGH
Clear, colored objects – such as tinted glass bottles or photographic slides – obtain their colors by subtracting some wavelengths from white light (pp. 32-33). Although shallow sea water sometimes looks transparent, sea water does absorb light. Red light is absorbed by the upper layers; blue and violet light penetrate farthest.

Color slides

Different parts of a color slide allow different wavelengths to pass through

Soap and beeswax let some light through, but the rays of light are scattered

This key reflects light but does not let it through

Opaque metal key

Blocking light

If a piece of aluminum foil is held up to a lamp, no light is seen, quite unlike the glow seen through a sheet of paper. This is because most metals are "opaque" – they do not let light pass through them. Some metals can let light through, but only if their atoms are formed into very thin layers. When you look at any opaque object, all the light you see is reflected by the object's surface. Shiny metals reflect nearly all the light that hits them, so they look bright. India ink reflects very little light, so it looks black.

Bottle of India ink

These painted scissors do not let light through but reflect red

Most of the light that strikes the ink is absorbed

Translucent soap

Translucent beeswax

Opaque scissors

Opaque wood bark

Opaque pyrites

47

Polarized light

NORMALLY, AN OBJECT SEEN through something transparent appears as a single image – but not always. In 1669 Erasmus Bartholin described how crystals of a mineral called Iceland spar (calcite) produce a double image. He rotated a crystal, and found one image moved while the other stayed put. In 1808 Etienne Malus, a French physicist, looked through Iceland spar under reflected light and found that one of the images had disappeared. He decided that ordinary daylight is made of two forms of light, which the crystal bent in different ways. At a certain angle, only one form of light was reflected by the mirror, so under reflected light only one image could be seen. It is now known that the difference between these forms of light lies in their "polarity," or nature of their waves (pp. 34-35). Daylight is usually "unpolarized" – its waves move up and down at all angles to its direction of movement. Reflected light is partially "polarized" – its waves move mainly in one plane.

PRESENTING A PUZZLE
In his book about Iceland spar, Erasmus Bartholin (1625-1698) described how its crystals split light in two different ways. This phenomenon is called double refraction, or birefringence.

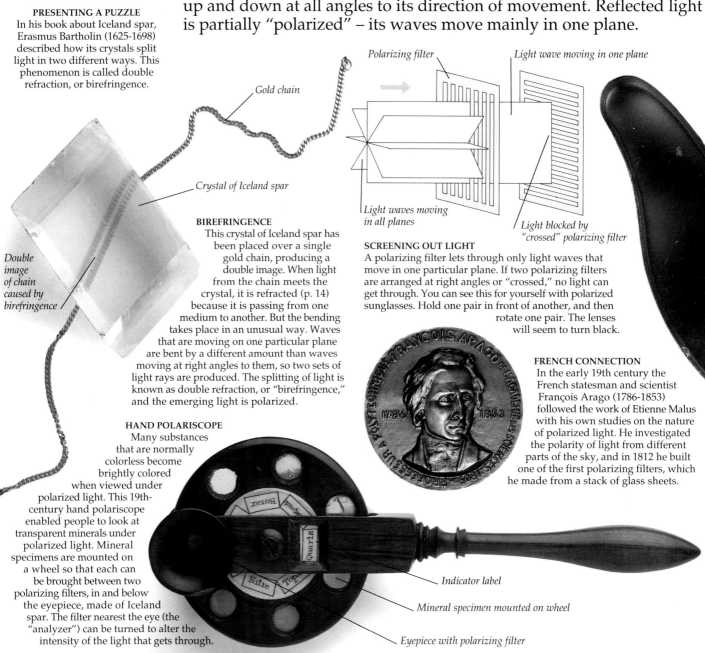

Gold chain

Crystal of Iceland spar

Double image of chain caused by birefringence

Polarizing filter

Light wave moving in one plane

Light waves moving in all planes

Light blocked by "crossed" polarizing filter

BIREFRINGENCE
This crystal of Iceland spar has been placed over a single gold chain, producing a double image. When light from the chain meets the crystal, it is refracted (p. 14) because it is passing from one medium to another. But the bending takes place in an unusual way. Waves that are moving on one particular plane are bent by a different amount than waves moving at right angles to them, so two sets of light rays are produced. The splitting of light is known as double refraction, or "birefringence," and the emerging light is polarized.

SCREENING OUT LIGHT
A polarizing filter lets through only light waves that move in one particular plane. If two polarizing filters are arranged at right angles or "crossed," no light can get through. You can see this for yourself with polarized sunglasses. Hold one pair in front of another, and then rotate one pair. The lenses will seem to turn black.

FRENCH CONNECTION
In the early 19th century the French statesman and scientist François Arago (1786-1853) followed the work of Etienne Malus with his own studies on the nature of polarized light. He investigated the polarity of light from different parts of the sky, and in 1812 he built one of the first polarizing filters, which he made from a stack of glass sheets.

HAND POLARISCOPE
Many substances that are normally colorless become brightly colored when viewed under polarized light. This 19th-century hand polariscope enabled people to look at transparent minerals under polarized light. Mineral specimens are mounted on a wheel so that each can be brought between two polarizing filters, in and below the eyepiece, made of Iceland spar. The filter nearest the eye (the "analyzer") can be turned to alter the intensity of the light that gets through.

Indicator label

Mineral specimen mounted on wheel

Eyepiece with polarizing filter

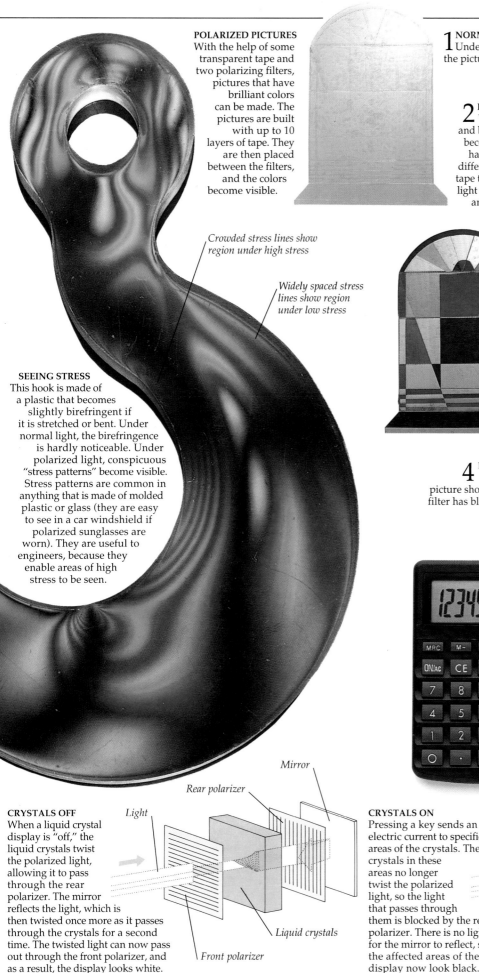

POLARIZED PICTURES
With the help of some transparent tape and two polarizing filters, pictures that have brilliant colors can be made. The pictures are built with up to 10 layers of tape. They are then placed between the filters, and the colors become visible.

1 NORMAL LIGHT
Under unpolarized light, the picture is transparent.

2 POLARIZED LIGHT
With filters in front and behind, the picture becomes colored. This happens because the different thicknesses of tape twist the polarized light waves by different amounts, according to their color.

Crowded stress lines show region under high stress

Widely spaced stress lines show region under low stress

3 ROTATING THE FILTER
If the front filter is turned, the colors change because the filter now cuts out different light waves.

SEEING STRESS
This hook is made of a plastic that becomes slightly birefringent if it is stretched or bent. Under normal light, the birefringence is hardly noticeable. Under polarized light, conspicuous "stress patterns" become visible. Stress patterns are common in anything that is made of molded plastic or glass (they are easy to see in a car windshield if polarized sunglasses are worn). They are useful to engineers, because they enable areas of high stress to be seen.

4 BLOCKING LIGHT
Black areas on the picture show where the front filter has blocked all the light.

LIQUID CRYSTAL DISPLAY (LCD)
A liquid crystal display contains two "crossed" polarizing filters backed by a mirror. Normally, crossed polarizers block all light, so the display should look black. But between the filters is a layer of liquid crystals. As long as the power is switched off, the crystals twist light rays through 90°. The twisted rays can then pass through the rear filter. They are reflected by the mirror, so the display looks white. The numbers or letters on a display are made by "switching on" areas of liquid crystals. This changes them so that they no longer twist the light.

CRYSTALS OFF
When a liquid crystal display is "off," the liquid crystals twist the polarized light, allowing it to pass through the rear polarizer. The mirror reflects the light, which is then twisted once more as it passes through the crystals for a second time. The twisted light can now pass out through the front polarizer, and as a result, the display looks white.

Mirror

Rear polarizer

Light

Liquid crystals

Front polarizer

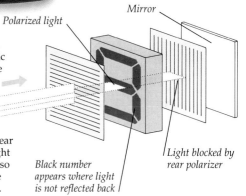

CRYSTALS ON
Pressing a key sends an electric current to specific areas of the crystals. The crystals in these areas no longer twist the polarized light, so the light that passes through them is blocked by the rear polarizer. There is no light for the mirror to reflect, so the affected areas of the display now look black.

Polarized light

Mirror

Black number appears where light is not reflected back

Light blocked by rear polarizer

Light energy

EVERY DAY THE EARTH is bathed by a huge amount of energy from the sun. In the course of a year, a single square yard of ground in a sunny part of the world receives over 2,000 kilowatt hours of light energy. If all this energy could be collected and converted into electricity, it would be enough to keep a kettle boiling non-stop for nearly six weeks. In the natural world a small part of the energy in sunlight is collected by the leaves of plants and used to fuel their growth. Recently, scientists have begun to look at ways in which humans can make use of the energy in light. Solar energy never runs out. It is cheap and non-polluting. However, collecting solar energy and converting it into a useful form is not easy, because at each step a large amount of the energy is lost. Mirrors in solar power stations waste energy when reflecting light, and solar cells can use only certain wavelengths. However, despite these drawbacks it seems certain that in the future solar energy will play a growing part in providing power.

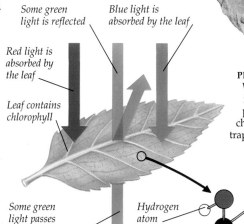

Some green light is reflected

Blue light is absorbed by the leaf

Red light is absorbed by the leaf

Leaf contains chlorophyll

Some green light passes through the leaf

Hydrogen atom

Carbon atom

Oxygen atom

Glucose molecule produced by photosynthesis

PLANTS AND OXYGEN
In 1771 English chemist Joseph Priestley (1733-1804) found that animals took in oxygen, but plants seemed to emit it. Eight years later Dutch doctor Jan Ingenhousz (1730-1799) investigated those findings and discovered that plants emit oxygen only when light shines on them. Ingenhousz's discovery was important because it showed that sunlight affects the chemical reactions that take place inside plants.

Jan Ingenhousz

PHOTOSYNTHESIS
When sunlight shines on a leaf, its energy is harnessed through a process called photosynthesis. This begins when chlorophyll, a chemical in the leaf's cells, traps the energy in sunlight. Chlorophyll passes this energy to other substances, and it is used to power a series of chemical reactions. During the day plants take in more carbon dioxide from the air than they give out. The energy from chlorophyll joins carbon dioxide with atoms of hydrogen to make a sugar called glucose. Glucose is an energy supply used for growth and a source of building materials for the walls of plant cells.

Solar cell panel used to power solar car

DRIVEN BY LIGHT
The Solar Flair is an experimental solar-powered car that can run at speeds of up to 40 mph (65 kph). Its streamlined body is made from a lightweight sandwich of aluminum honeycomb with a carbon-fiber composite material. It has nearly 900 solar cells arranged in panels on the top and rear of the car. The cells collect the energy in sunlight and convert it to electricity, which drives a special motor. In bright sunlight the cells can produce just over 1 kilowatt of power, or about 1.3 horsepower. (By comparison, the engine of a gasoline-driven car may produce over 100 horsepower.) Solar cars are still in their early days, and they may never be a practical proposition. However, many low-power devices, from telephones and calculators, work effectively on energy from the sun.

SOLAR CELLS
The cells that power the experimental solar car, Solar Flair, have no moving parts, so they need very little maintenance. Each one produces the same voltage as a flashlight battery. The cells are linked together in a line so that the small voltages add together to make a much bigger voltage.

When the light source is overhead, seedlings grow straight up

Cress seedlings

Motor

TURNED BY THE SUN
This small electric motor is driven by light energy falling on a solar cell. Solar cells work as a result of the photoelectric effect (p. 44). Instead of pushing electrons out of a metal, light falling on a solar cell is used to loosen electrons within a "semiconductor," usually silicon. The light energy arrives at the cell in packets, or photons, and these dislodge electrons within the silicon to create the current. The voltage produced across the cell depends on the wavelength of light that it uses. Green light gives electrons the same energy as a 2-volt battery. However, most solar cells are designed to work with light of longer wavelengths. Although they produce a lower voltage, they waste less of the light energy.

Solar cell

TURNING TO THE LIGHT
A plant cannot "see" sunlight, but it can grow toward it. If light shines on a plant from one side, that side of the plant's stem grows slowly, while the side away from the light grows more quickly. As a result, the stem bends. The cress seedlings here are growing toward the light. Together with some kinds of bacteria, plants are the only living things that can directly harness the energy of light. Animals obtain their energy by either eating plants or eating the animals that feed on plants.

When the source of light is to one side, the stems bend toward the light

POWER FROM THE SUN
Sunlight can be used by either gathering its heat energy or converting it directly into electricity. The sun's heat can be gathered by mirrors, which are focused onto a boiler to produce steam. This experimental solar power station in Sicily makes electricity with panels of solar cells. The panels can be turned so that they always point directly at the sun. Once a solar power station is in use, it creates little or no pollution.

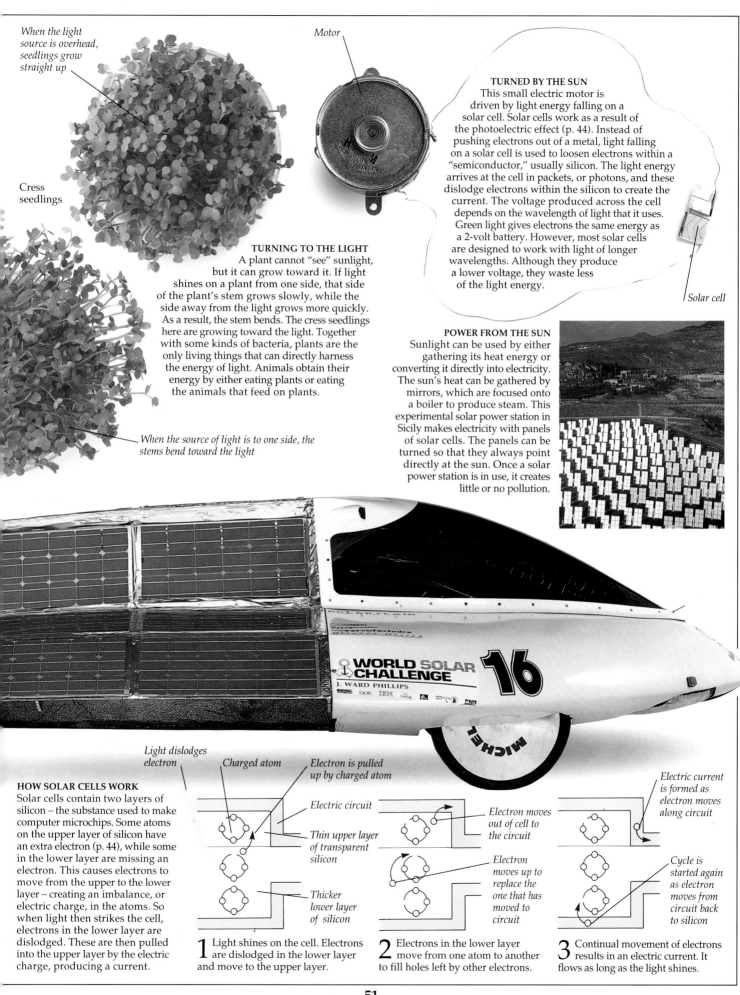

WORLD SOLAR CHALLENGE

J. WARD PHILLIPS

16

MICHEL

HOW SOLAR CELLS WORK
Solar cells contain two layers of silicon – the substance used to make computer microchips. Some atoms on the upper layer of silicon have an extra electron (p. 44), while some in the lower layer are missing an electron. This causes electrons to move from the upper to the lower layer – creating an imbalance, or electric charge, in the atoms. So when light then strikes the cell, electrons in the lower layer are dislodged. These are then pulled into the upper layer by the electric charge, producing a current.

Light dislodges electron

Charged atom

Electron is pulled up by charged atom

Electric circuit

Thin upper layer of transparent silicon

Thicker lower layer of silicon

1 Light shines on the cell. Electrons are dislodged in the lower layer and move to the upper layer.

Electron moves out of cell to the circuit

Electron moves up to replace the one that has moved to circuit

2 Electrons in the lower layer move from one atom to another to fill holes left by other electrons.

Electric current is formed as electron moves along circuit

Cycle is started again as electron moves from circuit back to silicon

3 Continual movement of electrons results in an electric current. It flows as long as the light shines.

Electric light

THE HISTORY OF practical electric lighting began in the early 1800s with the arc lamp. In this device, an electric current was made to jump across a small gap between two carbon rods. The light from arc lamps was much brighter than that from candles or gaslights, but arc lamps were difficult to install and were a fire hazard. In the mid 1870s the search began for ways to make a safe and reliable low-voltage electric light. Today, two men are credited with success in this venture. At practically the same time, Thomas Edison and Joseph Swan independently produced a new and different kind of lamp – the electric light bulb.

ELECTRIC BIRTHDAY
This illustration from an early 20th-century advertisement shows an unusual use for electric lighting.

Lights for all uses

Modern electric lamps produce light in three different ways. A normal light bulb works by "incandescence" – it glows because an electric current heats up its filament. In a fluorescent lamp the electric current flows through a gas that is under low pressure. The gas gives off ultraviolet light, and this strikes a phosphor coating, making it fluoresce (p. 45) and produce visible light. A vapor lamp contains a gas under low pressure, but the gas glows with visible light when electricity passes through it. The color of the light depends on the type of gas.

SWAN'S LAMP
Joseph Swan demonstrated his lamp in Britain in February 1879. It had a carbon filament, which glowed when a current flowed through it. The glass "bulb" contained a partial vacuum. There was so little oxygen in the bulb that the filament could get very hot without catching fire.

Partial vacuum

Carbon filament made from a specially treated thread

Partial vacuum

Filament made of a single loop of carbon

Edison's lamp

Joseph Wilson Swan (1828-1914)

Swan's lamp

DAYLIGHT BULB
This filament bulb is designed to imitate natural daylight. Its light is actually made up of a broad mixture of colors, just like light from the sun. In this light, the colored walls around the bulb appear as they would in daylight.

EDISON'S LAMP
This lamp made by Thomas Edison (1847-1931) was demonstrated in the United States in October 1879, and it went into commercial production in November 1880. It had reduced oxygen to keep the filament from burning. It quickly became popular. Some hotels had to remind guests they did not need matches to light the new lamps.

Art gallery lit with Edison lamps

THE GEISSLER TUBE
In the mid 1850s Johann Heinrich Wilhelm Geissler made tubes that contained gases at low pressure. It was known that passing electricity through them caused a colored glow. These tubes were the forerunners of today's streetlights and neon signs.

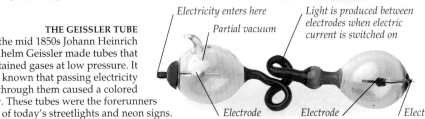

Electricity enters here

Partial vacuum

Light is produced between electrodes when electric current is switched on

Electrode

Electrode

Electricity passes through here

MERCURY LAMP *(left)*
A mercury vapor lamp makes the left wall look blue, but the right turns a blue-gray. This is because the light contains no red, so the right wall cannot reflect it. The light does contain some yellow, so the bottom wall still reflects a bit of this color.

STANDARD LIGHT BULB *(below)*
An ordinary light bulb contains about 20 in (50 cm) of coiled tungsten filament surrounded by inert gases, such as argon, at low pressure. The filament emits a yellowish-white light. Only about 8 percent of the electrical energy is converted to light.

LOW-PRESSURE SODIUM LAMP *(above)*
This kind of lamp is also used for street lighting. It contains a small amount of sodium, which takes a few minutes to vaporize when the lamp is switched on. The colors around this lamp show that its light is an almost pure yellow.

HIGH-PRESSURE SODIUM LAMP *(left)*
These are used for street lighting in cities. They contain sodium and aluminum, which combine to make pinkish-blue light. This gives most objects a similar color as daylight. These lamps are quite efficient at converting electricity to light.

Total internal reflection

WHEN YOU LOOK INTO A MIRROR, you always see a reflection. This shows that the mirror reflects light rays arriving from all angles. But light can also be reflected in another way. In total internal reflection, light is reflected from some angles but not others. To understand this, think of a diver working underwater at night equipped with a powerful flashlight. The water's surface above is perfectly calm. If the diver points the flashlight straight up, the beam will shine out of the water and vertically into the air. If the flashlight is turned slightly to one side, the beam will no longer hit the surface at right angles. It will still shine into the air, but this time refraction (p. 14) will bend it so that the light makes a smaller angle to the water's surface. If the diver keeps slanting the beam down, it will meet the surface at a smaller and smaller angle. Refraction will bend it further and further. Eventually, the emerging light will be bent so far that it will be parallel to the water's surface. At this point the water's "critical angle" will be reached. If the flashlight is turned a little more, refraction stops altogether, and the water's surface becomes a mirror. Instead of letting the light out, it reflects it back down again. This is the principle behind fiber optics.

Internal reflection works around even gradual bends

Light ray

Prism focuses the light

The light rays are internally reflected if they hit the sides of the bar at a shallow angle

TRAPPING LIGHT
Here a beam of light is reflected by a bar of clear plastic. The reflection is "total" because little or no light escapes from the bar during each reflection. It is "internal" because the all the reflections take place inside the bar. This kind of reflection happens only under particular conditions. The light must be traveling inside a medium with a high refractive index (p. 14), such as water, glass, or plastic. This must be surrounded by a medium with a lower refractive index, such as air. The light must also hit the boundary between the two at a shallow angle.

No light escapes when the beam is reflected

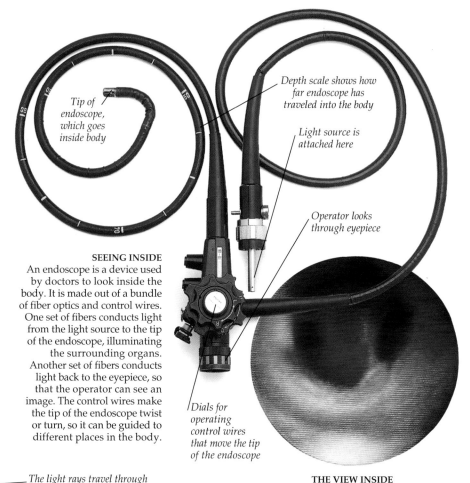

Tip of endoscope, which goes inside body

Depth scale shows how far endoscope has traveled into the body

Light source is attached here

Operator looks through eyepiece

SEEING INSIDE
An endoscope is a device used by doctors to look inside the body. It is made out of a bundle of fiber optics and control wires. One set of fibers conducts light from the light source to the tip of the endoscope, illuminating the surrounding organs. Another set of fibers conducts light back to the eyepiece, so that the operator can see an image. The control wires make the tip of the endoscope twist or turn, so it can be guided to different places in the body.

Dials for operating control wires that move the tip of the endoscope

The light rays travel through the end of the bar because they strike it at a steep angle

THE VIEW INSIDE
The view of an artery through an endoscope is made out of small points of light from the separate fibers. These build up an image in the same way that an image is formed by an insect's eye (p. 19).

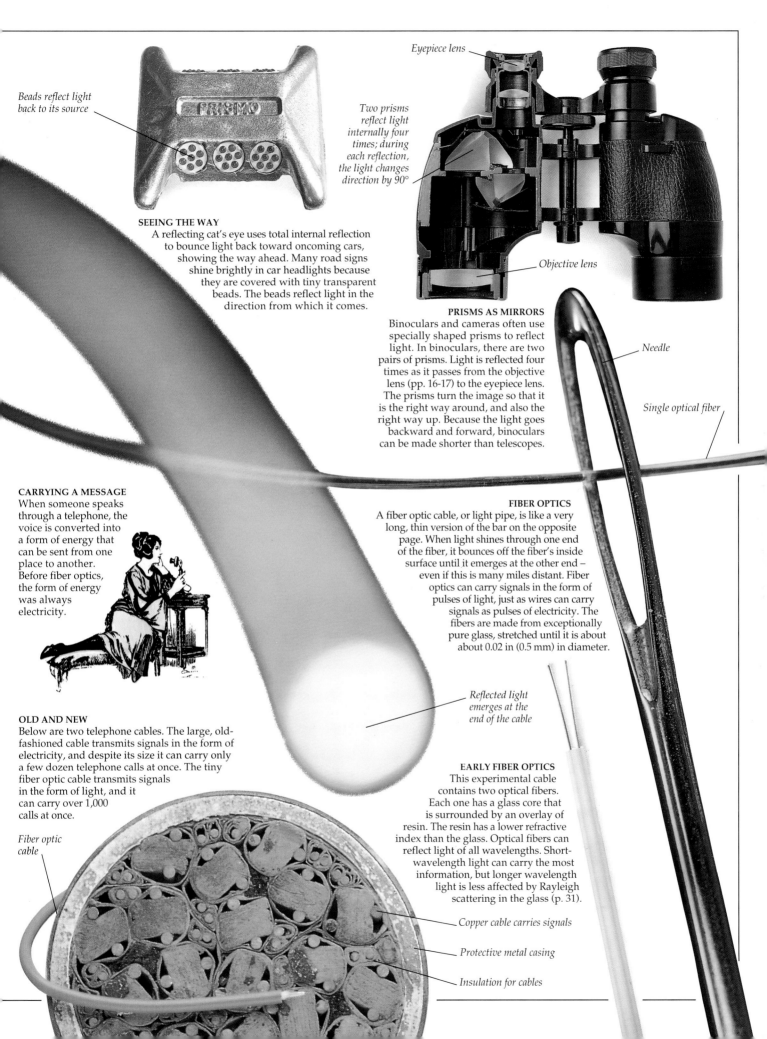

Beads reflect light back to its source

Eyepiece lens

Two prisms reflect light internally four times; during each reflection, the light changes direction by 90°

Objective lens

SEEING THE WAY
A reflecting cat's eye uses total internal reflection to bounce light back toward oncoming cars, showing the way ahead. Many road signs shine brightly in car headlights because they are covered with tiny transparent beads. The beads reflect light in the direction from which it comes.

PRISMS AS MIRRORS
Binoculars and cameras often use specially shaped prisms to reflect light. In binoculars, there are two pairs of prisms. Light is reflected four times as it passes from the objective lens (pp. 16-17) to the eyepiece lens. The prisms turn the image so that it is the right way around, and also the right way up. Because the light goes backward and forward, binoculars can be made shorter than telescopes.

Needle

Single optical fiber

CARRYING A MESSAGE
When someone speaks through a telephone, the voice is converted into a form of energy that can be sent from one place to another. Before fiber optics, the form of energy was always electricity.

FIBER OPTICS
A fiber optic cable, or light pipe, is like a very long, thin version of the bar on the opposite page. When light shines through one end of the fiber, it bounces off the fiber's inside surface until it emerges at the other end – even if this is many miles distant. Fiber optics can carry signals in the form of pulses of light, just as wires can carry signals as pulses of electricity. The fibers are made from exceptionally pure glass, stretched until it is about about 0.02 in (0.5 mm) in diameter.

OLD AND NEW
Below are two telephone cables. The large, old-fashioned cable transmits signals in the form of electricity, and despite its size it can carry only a few dozen telephone calls at once. The tiny fiber optic cable transmits signals in the form of light, and it can carry over 1,000 calls at once.

Reflected light emerges at the end of the cable

Fiber optic cable

EARLY FIBER OPTICS
This experimental cable contains two optical fibers. Each one has a glass core that is surrounded by an overlay of resin. The resin has a lower refractive index than the glass. Optical fibers can reflect light of all wavelengths. Short-wavelength light can carry the most information, but longer wavelength light is less affected by Rayleigh scattering in the glass (p. 31).

Copper cable carries signals

Protective metal casing

Insulation for cables

Laser light

THE LIGHT THAT WE SEE IS USUALLY a mixture of many different wavelengths, or colors. Because atoms normally give off light at random, the light waves that they produce are also out of step. These two factors mean that ordinary light is a mixture of many different types of waves. But laser light is different. Instead of containing many wavelengths, it contains just one. Not only this, but the waves are also "coherent," meaning that they are are all exactly in step with one another. Laser light is made by feeding energy into a solid, liquid, or gas. As the substance takes in energy, its atoms start to release light of a particular wavelength. When light from one atom strikes its neighbors more light is released, and this chain reaction continues until many atoms are emitting light all at the same time. This light is reflected by special mirrors so that it surges backward and forward within the laser. Eventually the light becomes so intense that some of it passes through one of the mirrors and forms a laser beam.

THE FIRST LASER
The word laser stands for "Light Amplification by Stimulated Emission of Radiation." The first working laser was built in 1960 by Theodore Maiman, shown here pouring coolant into an early experimental model. It was built around a cylinder of synthetic ruby, surrounded by a spiral lamp. Maiman's laser was only a few inches long, but it worked very successfully. Since Maiman made his laser, many different uses have been found for its intense and organized light.

HELIUM-NEON LASER
This laser makes light by feeding an electric current through a tube containing helium and neon gases. The energy is passed to the helium atoms, which collide with the neon atoms – making them produce light. At the ends of the tube are two mirrors. One reflects light, but the other lets a small amount through so that the laser beam can emerge.

Power supply "excites" the light-producing substance

Laser light is reflected by the fully silvered mirror

Electrodes are the power supply producing a continuous electric discharge through the gas mixture

HOW LASER LIGHT WORKS
To make a laser beam, many atoms or molecules must be "excited" – given enough energy so that they reach high-energy states. They can then release light, which bounces back and forth in the light-producing substance. The intensity of the beam rises every time light travels from one end of the substance to another. The light escapes through a hole in one mirror, or through a mirror that lets through a small amount of light.

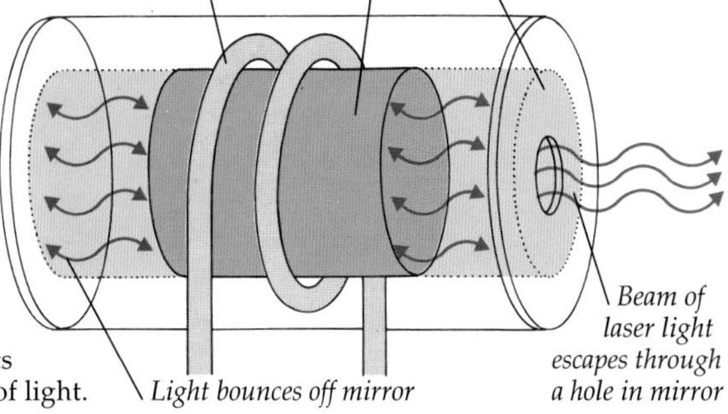

"Excited" substance releases light

Light bounces off this mirror to other mirror

Beam of laser light escapes through a hole in mirror

Light bounces off mirror

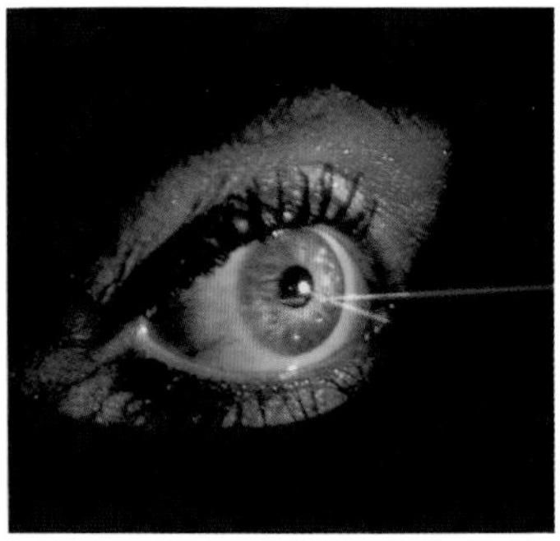

LIFESAVERS
If part of the eye's retina (p. 18) comes loose, the eye can no longer see clearly. A helium-neon laser beam can be shone through the pupil to weld the retina back in position. Laser beams are used by surgeons to cut or weld other parts of the body with great accuracy.

RUBY LASER

This ruby laser was made in the mid 1960s. It contains a long rod of synthetic ruby, which lies next to a lamp when the unit is closed and ready for use. The mirror like surface on the inside of the laser ensures that the ruby is bombarded with as much light as possible. The light produces a large amount of heat, so some lasers have a built-in water cooling system. Ruby lasers produce red light with a wavelength of about 695 nm.

Laser beam emerges through end of ruby rod

Rod of synthetic ruby

Laser light is produced by chromium atoms within the ruby

Reflecting surface

High-intensity lamp

Tube containing helium and neon at low pressure

DEADLY LIGHT

At one time deadly rays of light were no more than science fiction – in the 1958 film, *Colossus of New York*, a monster with the brain of a dead scientist emitted lethal light rays from his eyes. But with the invention of the laser, it really is possible to make a beam of light that can destroy objects at great distances. Unlike ordinary light, a laser beam does not spread out, so it can be aimed very precisely.

Most of the light is reflected by the semi-silvered mirror, but a small amount passes straight through and emerges as the laser beam

The narrow red laser beam consists of coherent light with a wavelength of about 694 nm

MADE TO MEASURE

Laser beams always follow a straight line, so they are often used in engineering projects, such as tunneling, to ensure the work is following the right course. Laser light can also be used to measure very small distances. This is done by using the interference (pp. 36-37) that is produced when a laser beam is split and then reflected back by different surfaces. By then analyzing interference fringes, the distance between two objects can be calculated very accurately.

CUTTING WITH LIGHT

Long-wavelength lasers can be directed onto a surface to produce intense heat in a very small area. This heat can cut through materials of all kinds, from fabrics for clothing to steel plates used for building cars. Laser heat can also be used in spot welding, when two pieces of metal are glued together by making them melt. One advantage of a laser beam is that it does not become blunt like ordinary cutting tools, which must be sharpened or replaced.

Holograms

A PHOTOGRAPH RECORDS the intensity of light that falls on film (pp. 24-25). It is made by one set of light waves, and the image that the light waves form is flat, or two-dimensional. A hologram is different. It is taken in laser light, and instead of being made by one set of light waves it is made by two. One set of waves is reflected onto the film by the object, just as ordinary light waves are in a photograph. The other set of waves arrives at the film from a different direction without meeting the object at all. Where the two sets of waves meet each other, they produce interference fringes (p. 38) that are recorded in the film. When the hologram is viewed, these interference fringes produce a three-dimensional image.

THEORY AND PRACTICE
Dennis Gabor (1900-1979), shown here in a transmission hologram, outlined the principle of holography in 1948. He realized that a beam of light could be split to produce a three-dimensional image. But Gabor's holography needed a source of light waves that were "coherent," or in step. This did not appear until 1960 with the invention of the laser. In 1962 the first successful hologram was made by two Americans, Juris Upatnieks and Emmet Leith.

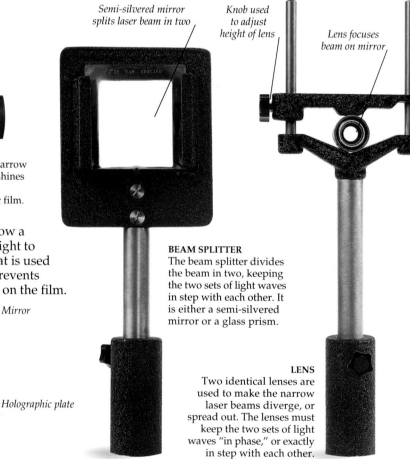

Helium-neon laser fires a beam at the beam splitter

Semi-silvered mirror splits laser beam in two

Knob used to adjust height of lens

Lens focuses beam on mirror

Transmission holograms

Transmission holograms are viewed in laser light. The diagram below shows how a transmission hologram is made by splitting laser light to form two separate beams. All of the equipment that is used (right) is mounted on a special heavy table. This prevents vibrations that could blur the interference fringes on the film.

HELIUM-NEON LASER
This laser produces a narrow beam of red light that shines for several minutes to expose the holographic film.

BEAM SPLITTER
The beam splitter divides the beam in two, keeping the two sets of light waves in step with each other. It is either a semi-silvered mirror or a glass prism.

LENS
Two identical lenses are used to make the narrow laser beams diverge, or spread out. The lenses must keep the two sets of light waves "in phase," or exactly in step with each other.

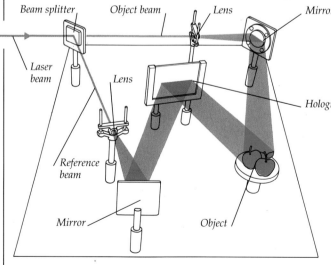

Beam splitter   *Object beam*   *Lens*   *Mirror*

Laser beam

Lens

Holographic plate

Reference beam

Mirror   *Object*

LIGHT PATH IN TRANSMISSION HOLOGRAPHY
The laser beam is split. The "object" beam passes through a lens and is reflected onto the object. Its light then shines onto the holographic plate, coated with photographic emulsion. The "reference" beam passes through a lens and is reflected onto the emulsion, where it meets light from the object beam and produces interference fringes.

Reflection holograms

A reflection hologram is made by shining a reference beam and an object beam onto a thick film from opposite sides. The beams interfere to produce tiny areas of light and dark throughout the film. When the hologram is viewed, this pattern reflects light in a way that produces a three-dimensional image.

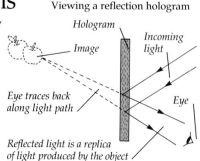

Viewing a reflection hologram

Hologram

Image

Incoming light

Eye

Eye traces back along light path

Reflected light is a replica of light produced by the object

58

MAKING A TRANSMISSION HOLOGRAM

A transmission hologram is made by two sets of laser waves that strike the same side of a special photographic emulsion. One set of waves is produced by the object beam, which here illuminates two apples. The apples reflect the waves, scattering them in the same way that they would scatter waves of ordinary daylight. The scattered waves spread outward from the apples until they reach the emulsion. At the same time, the waves from the reference beam also reach the emulsion. The two sets of waves then interfere with each other. Where two waves are in step, they produce a point of bright light. Where they are exactly out of step, they produce darkness. The emulsion records the pattern of light and darkness that interference creates.

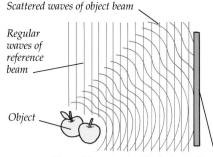

Scattered waves of object beam

Regular waves of reference beam

Object

Glass plate covered with photographic emulsion captures interference patterns

VIEWING A TRANSMISSION HOLOGRAM

Seen by daylight, a transmission hologram looks blank because the interference fringes on it are far too small to be seen. But if the hologram is illuminated by the reference beam, an image appears. This happens because the interference fringes in the film affect the laser light. They interfere with the laser beam in a way that "reconstructs" the original waves of light that were scattered by the apples. The reconstructed waves are exactly the same as those that would have been produced by the apples if the hologram was not there. The result is a three-dimensional image – one that changes according to the angle from which it is viewed.

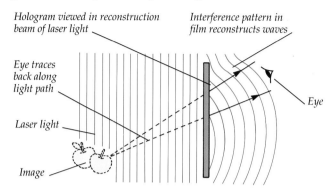

Hologram viewed in reconstruction beam of laser light

Interference pattern in film reconstructs waves

Eye traces back along light path

Laser light

Eye

Image

Holographic mirror reflects light on to object or holographic plate

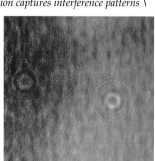

INTERFERENCE PATTERNS
The interference patterns in a transmission hologram are made of microscopic light and dark areas. They form an image only when the hologram is viewed in front of laser light of the correct wavelength.

Object to be shown in hologram

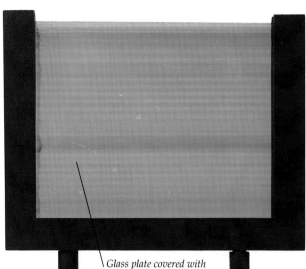

Glass plate covered with photographic emulsion

MIRROR
Two mirrors are used to bring the beams together so they interfere. The silvering on each mirror lies on the surface. This ensures that the beams are not refracted (p. 14) by traveling through the glass.

OBJECT
The object sits in a heavy plinth that helps prevent vibration. Most holograms need a long exposure time, so it is essential that the object keeps completely still.

HOLOGRAPHIC PLATE
The "film" in a transmission hologram is usually a glass plate coated with a special photographic emulsion. It has a fine grain used to record interference fringes that are far too small to be seen with the naked eye.

SECURITY HOLOGRAMS
Unlike transmission holograms, reflection holograms can be used in daylight. They are often used on credit cards to prevent forgery. They show color images, produced using laser light of the three primary colors (p. 30). Each laser wavelength produces its own interference pattern, and the patterns add together to give a color image. These holograms are almost impossible to copy, so they are a valuable security device.

HEAD-UP DISPLAY
In a traditional aircraft cockpit the pilot can either look out of the windows or down at the controls. With a "heads-up display," the pilot can look at both at the same time. A three-dimensional transmission hologram is made, and reflected by the cockpit window. Here it is used in a fighter plane to show the target.

The speed of light

IN ANCIENT TIMES most people thought that the speed of light was infinite. Once the scientific study of light began, opinions slowly changed. Alhazen (p. 12) thought that light traveled very rapidly but still had a definite speed. The first estimate of the speed of light was made in 1675 by a Danish astronomer, Ole Roemer. Roemer had been watching the movement of Jupiter's moons, and he had noticed that the times they appeared and vanished seemed to vary throughout the year. He guessed that this was because the distance from the earth to Jupiter changed during a yearly cycle, and that so did the distance that the light had to travel. By some simple mathematics, Roemer estimated the speed of light to be about 137,000 miles (220,000 km) per second. The first land-based estimate was not made until 1849, by Armand Fizeau. Fizeau's figure, and the one calculated a year later by Léon Foucault, showed that Roemer's estimate was too low. Today, the speed of light in a vacuum is known to be almost exactly 186,000 miles (300,000 km) per second.

TRAVELING LIGHT
Ole Roemer (1644-1710) recorded the time it took Jupiter's moons to circle their planet. He noticed that at certain times of the year the moons seemed to be slightly ahead or behind their expected timetable. Over a year the difference was about 22 minutes. Roemer realized this must be caused by the changing distance the light traveled from Jupiter to the earth. He knew the radius of the earth's orbit around the sun, so he could calculate the change in the distance the light had to travel. This led to the first close estimate of the speed of light.

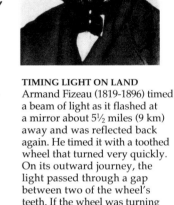

TIMING LIGHT ON LAND
Armand Fizeau (1819-1896) timed a beam of light as it flashed at a mirror about 5½ miles (9 km) away and was reflected back again. He timed it with a toothed wheel that turned very quickly. On its outward journey, the light passed through a gap between two of the wheel's teeth. If the wheel was turning fast enough, the light could pass through the neighboring gap on its return journey. By knowing the wheel's speed, Fizeau could calculate the speed of light.

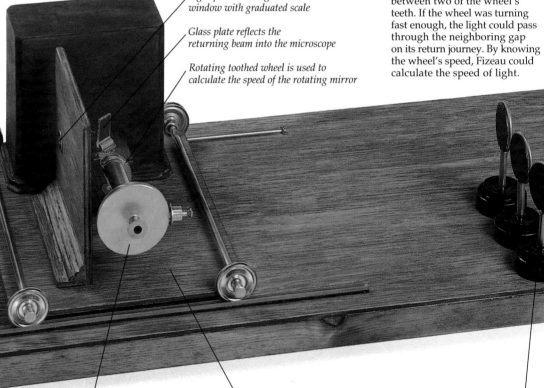

Light passes through window with graduated scale

Glass plate reflects the returning beam into the microscope

Rotating toothed wheel is used to calculate the speed of the rotating mirror

Light enters through hole

Foucault's speed of light experiment

The shift of the light beam is measured by observing the image of the graduated scale through the microscope

The glass plate and microscope are mounted on a trolley so the distance the light travels can be adjusted

Stationary concave mirrors reflect the light in a zig-zag path

THE MOONS OF JUPITER

Jupiter is the biggest planet in the solar system, and it has at least 16 moons. As each of these moons travels around the giant planet, it moves in and out of "eclipse." This was first noted by Galileo (p. 20), and it was used by Roemer to determine the speed of light. This photograph, taken in 1979 by the Voyager 1 spacecraft, shows two of the "Galilean" moons – Io (in front of the planet) and Europa (to the right).

1 second

Speed of light in a vacuum 186,000 miles (300,000 km) per second; refractive index of air 1

Speed of light in water 140,000 miles (225,000 km) per second; refractive index of water 1.3

Speed of light in glass 124,000 miles (200,000 km) per second; refractive index of glass 1.5

Speed of light in diamond 77,500 miles (125,000 km) per second; refractive index of diamond 2.4

THE VARYING SPEED OF LIGHT

Armand Fizeau's method of calculating the speed of light relied on a very long light path to give an accurate result. For this reason it could be used only in air. In Foucault's method, shown below, the light path was much shorter. This allowed Foucault to test the speed of light in transparent substances other than air. He found that light's speed in water or glass was only about two-thirds of its speed in air. He also discovered that the speed of light was related to the substance's refractive index (pp. 14-15). The more the substance bent light, the slower the light traveled. This finding was exactly what the wave theory of light had predicted (p. 35).

FOUCAULT'S SPINNING MIRROR (below)

Léon Foucault, who worked with Fizeau, devised a way of measuring the speed of light that used a spinning mirror. In his experiment a beam of light passed through a graduated scale and then struck the spinning mirror. The spinning mirror reflected the light to a series of stationary mirrors, which made the beam follow a zig-zag path. By the time the light had completed this journey and returned to the spinning mirror, the mirror had turned very slightly. It reflected the beam back toward its source, but along a slightly different path. Foucault's apparatus was arranged so that this tiny shift in the light path could be seen and measured. Foucault knew the distance that the light had travelled and the speed of the mirror. By combining these with the shift, he obtained a figure of about 185,000 miles (298,000 km) per second for light traveling in air.

A lens focuses the light on the spinning mirror

The mirror is turned at high speed by a compressed air turbine

LEON FOUCAULT

Léon Foucault (1819-1868) calculated the speed of light in air and water. He also invented the gyroscope and used the movement of a giant pendulum to demonstrate that the earth is rotating.

Stationary concave mirrors reflect the light in a zig-zag path

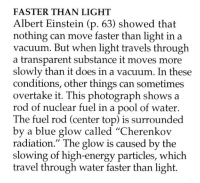

FASTER THAN LIGHT

Albert Einstein (p. 63) showed that nothing can move faster than light in a vacuum. But when light travels through a transparent substance it moves more slowly than it does in a vacuum. In these conditions, other things can sometimes overtake it. This photograph shows a rod of nuclear fuel in a pool of water. The fuel rod (center top) is surrounded by a blue glow called "Cherenkov radiation." The glow is caused by the slowing of high-energy particles, which travel through water faster than light.

Path of light in Foucault's experiment

DOUBLING BACK

In Foucault's experiment the light beam was shone through a graduated scale. It passed straight through a glass plate angled at 45° to the light beam. On the return journey the glass plate acted as a mirror and reflected the beam into a microscope. Here the image of the scale could be seen in the beam, and its sideways shift measured. Foucault's apparatus also included a toothed wheel, which was used for checking the speed of the mirror.

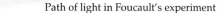

The total length of the light path is about 66 ft (20 m)

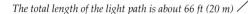

Light in space

DURING THE 19TH century most scientists thought "empty" space was not actually empty at all. Like Christian Huygens (p. 34), they believed it was filled with a substance called the "luminiferous ether." They thought light waves moved through the ether, as did the stars and planets. According to this theory the ether was invisible, frictionless, and absolutely still. In 1887 two American physicists, Albert Michelson and Edward Morley, tried to use interference (p. 36) to find out how fast the earth moved through the ether. But despite many attempts they were unable to detect any movement. In 1905 this perplexing result was explained by Albert Einstein in his Special Theory of Relativity. Einstein believed that all movement was relative. There could be no such thing as absolute movement, because there was nothing absolutely still to measure it against. His theory spelled the end for the ether, and today scientists believe that light can travel through nothingness itself.

LIGHT FROM ABOVE
In medieval times, people thought that the stars were fixed in the sky, and that the earth was the center of the universe. With the development of astronomy, it became clear that the stars were much farther away than was first thought. Today, measurement of starlight using spectroscopes shows that most galaxies (large groups of stars) are moving away from us at great speed.

Microscope used to view interference fringes on the semi-silvered mirror

Mirrors to reflect light beams

Adjustable mirror for altering length of light path

The Michelson–Morley experiment

The principle behind this experiment is simple. A beam of light is split in two, and the two beams are made to travel at right angles to each other by a set of mirrors. If the earth is moving through the ether, whichever beam is traveling back and forth across the flow of ether will have farther to go. This means that the waves in the two beams should become slightly out of step. When the two beams are brought together again, this should produce interference fringes (p. 36). The faster the earth moves, the more out of step the waves should be. This is what the experiment was expected to show. Michelson and Morley designed the apparatus to ensure that the tiniest difference between the two sets of waves would produce a noticeable result.

ALBERT MICHELSON
With Edward Morley (1838-1923), Albert Michelson (1852-1931) tried to use interference to investigate earth's movement in space.

A WEB OF LIGHT
In the Michelson–Morley experiment the light beams were shone back and forth on a slowly, steadily turning slab. The beam was first split in two by a semi-silvered mirror. The two beams were then reflected by mirrors and joined again. The light could then be examined through a microscope. As the slab turned, the observer could check to see if interference fringes were visible. None were ever seen.

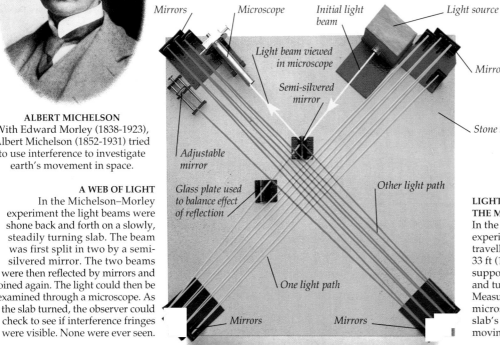

Mirrors   *Microscope*   *Initial light beam*   *Light source*

Light beam viewed in microscope

Semi-silvered mirror

Mirrors

Stone slab

Adjustable mirror

Glass plate used to balance effect of reflection

Other light path

One light path

Mirrors   *Mirrors*

LIGHT ON THE MOVE (right)
In the Michelson–Morley experiment the light beam travelled a distance of over 33 ft (10 m). The stone slab that supported the apparatus was 5 sq ft (1.5 sq m) and turned about once every 6 minutes. Measurements were taken by using the moving microscope. The pool of mercury made the slab's motion almost frictionless, so, once moving, the slab took hours to come to a halt.

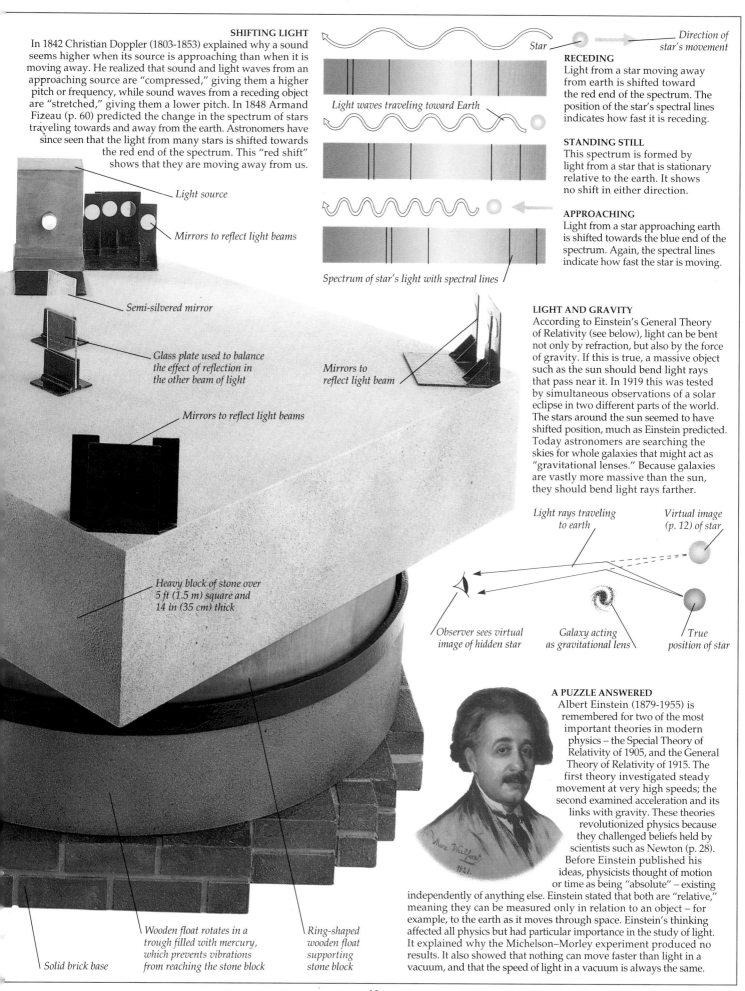

SHIFTING LIGHT

In 1842 Christian Doppler (1803-1853) explained why a sound seems higher when its source is approaching than when it is moving away. He realized that sound and light waves from an approaching source are "compressed," giving them a higher pitch or frequency, while sound waves from a receding object are "stretched," giving them a lower pitch. In 1848 Armand Fizeau (p. 60) predicted the change in the spectrum of stars traveling towards and away from the earth. Astronomers have since seen that the light from many stars is shifted towards the red end of the spectrum. This "red shift" shows that they are moving away from us.

Light source

Mirrors to reflect light beams

Semi-silvered mirror

Glass plate used to balance the effect of reflection in the other beam of light

Mirrors to reflect light beams

Mirrors to reflect light beam

Heavy block of stone over 5 ft (1.5 m) square and 14 in (35 cm) thick

Wooden float rotates in a trough filled with mercury, which prevents vibrations from reaching the stone block

Ring-shaped wooden float supporting stone block

Solid brick base

Light waves traveling toward Earth

Spectrum of star's light with spectral lines

Star

Direction of star's movement

RECEDING

Light from a star moving away from earth is shifted toward the red end of the spectrum. The position of the star's spectral lines indicates how fast it is receding.

STANDING STILL

This spectrum is formed by light from a star that is stationary relative to the earth. It shows no shift in either direction.

APPROACHING

Light from a star approaching earth is shifted towards the blue end of the spectrum. Again, the spectral lines indicate how fast the star is moving.

LIGHT AND GRAVITY

According to Einstein's General Theory of Relativity (see below), light can be bent not only by refraction, but also by the force of gravity. If this is true, a massive object such as the sun should bend light rays that pass near it. In 1919 this was tested by simultaneous observations of a solar eclipse in two different parts of the world. The stars around the sun seemed to have shifted position, much as Einstein predicted. Today astronomers are searching the skies for whole galaxies that might act as "gravitational lenses." Because galaxies are vastly more massive than the sun, they should bend light rays farther.

Light rays traveling to earth

Virtual image (p. 12) of star

Observer sees virtual image of hidden star

Galaxy acting as gravitational lens

True position of star

A PUZZLE ANSWERED

Albert Einstein (1879-1955) is remembered for two of the most important theories in modern physics – the Special Theory of Relativity of 1905, and the General Theory of Relativity of 1915. The first theory investigated steady movement at very high speeds; the second examined acceleration and its links with gravity. These theories revolutionized physics because they challenged beliefs held by scientists such as Newton (p. 28). Before Einstein published his ideas, physicists thought of motion or time as being "absolute" – existing independently of anything else. Einstein stated that both are "relative," meaning they can be measured only in relation to an object – for example, to the earth as it moves through space. Einstein's thinking affected all physics but had particular importance in the study of light. It explained why the Michelson–Morley experiment produced no results. It also showed that nothing can move faster than light in a vacuum, and that the speed of light in a vacuum is always the same.

Index

Acknowledgments

Dorling Kindersley would like to thank:
Jane Wess of the Science Museum for checking the text; Fred Archer, Tim Boon, Brian Bowers, Roger Bridgman, Neil Brown, Robert Bud, Sue Cackett, Ian Carter, Ann Carter, Tony Clarke, Helen Dowling, Stewart Emmens, Robert Excell, Graeme Fyffe, Colin Harding, Derek Hudson, Stephanie Millard, Kate Morris, David Ray and his staff, Derek Robinson, Victoria Smith, Peter Stephens, Peter Tomlinson, Tony Vincent, Anthony Wilson, and David Woodcock for advice and help with the provision of objects for photography at the Science Museum; Peter Griffiths for model making; Deborah Rhodes for page makeup; Jane Bull for design assistance; Susannah Steel for

editorial assistance; Karl Adamson and Jonathan Buckley for additional photography and assistance; Jack Challoner and Neil Ardley for consulting on the text; Fiona Spence of De Beers for the loan of cubic zirconias; British Telecom for the provision of fiber optics; Stephen Herbert for the loan of the magic lantern; Lester Smith for the loan of the magic lantern burner; Phil Farrand for allowing photography of the solar car; Mike Bartley for the loan of the shadow theater.

Picture research Deborah Pownall and Catherine O'Rourke
Illustrations Kuo Kang Chen, Janos Marffy, Alistair Wardle, and John Woodcock
Index Jane Parker

Picture credits

t=top b=bottom c=center l=left r=right

Ardea 6bl. Associated Press 56tl. Bibliotheque d'Arsenal, Paris 62tc. Bridgeman Art Library 8tl; 12tr. Paul Brierley 36cl; 59tlc. BT Museum, London 42cl. Bulloz/Institut de France, Paris 10bc. David Burnie 33tl. Jean-Loup Charmet 60cr. Bruce Coleman 19br. Ken Day 10tl. Mary Evans Picture Library 6cl; 6bc; 11bl; 20tr; 52tl; 63bm. Werner Foreman 7tr; 7cr. Sonia Halliday 29tl. Colorphoto Hinz 32tr. Michael Holford 12tl. Hulton Picture Co. 14tl; 14br; 44cl; 44cr. Kobal Collection 57tr. Mansell Collection 32c. National Maritime Museum, London 8cr. National Physical Laboratory, Teddington 37br. National Portrait Gallery, London 33c. Ann Ronan Picture Library 8cl; 8bc; 10cb; 22tr; 48cr; 62cl. Scala 19c. Science Museum Photo Library, London

cover front cr; back cl; 10bl; 11tl; 17br; 24tr; 25cl; 26tr; 27tr; 28cl; 36cr; 52bl; 52br; 53clb; 53br; 58tl. Science Photo Library 15tr; 18br; /Barney McGrath 20tl; /John Sanford 21tr; 29bl; 31tl; 33c; 41tr; 43bl; /John Stevenson 43br; 44br; 45cr; /Philippe Plailly 51cr; /Alexander Tsiaras 56br: /Philip Plailly 59bl; 61tl; 61cr. Ian Whitelaw 7c. Zefa 6tl; 25br; /Tom Ives 42bc; /John Earle 42br; /Bramaz 57bc; /Tom Tracey 57br; /Armstrong Roberts 59br.

With the exception of the items listed above, and objects on pages 6-7c, 10-11 cr and tr, 12-13 c, 14tr, 26-27c, 38-39 (except the Newton's Rings), 40-41, 42-43, 45t, 46-47, 60-61, 62-63, all the photographs in this book are of objects in the collections of the Science Museum, London.